ABOUT THE AUTHOR

Richard Glover is the author of ten books, including the bestsellers *In Bed with Jocasta*, *The Dag's Dictionary* and *Desperate Husbands*. He writes a weekly column for the *Sydney Morning Herald* and presents the Drive show on ABC Radio in Sydney. To find out more, please visit

www.richardglover.com.au

Also by Richard Glover

Grin and Bear It

The P-Plate Parent
(with Angela Webber)

Laughing Stock

The Joy of Blokes
(with Angela Webber)

In Bed with Jocasta

The Dag's Dictionary

Desperate Husbands

For children

The Dirt Experiment

The Joke Trap

The No-Minute Noodler

The Mud House

The Mud House

FOUR FRIENDS
ONE BLOCK OF LAND
NO POWER TOOLS

RICHARD GLOVER

HarperCollins*Publishers*

HarperCollins*Publishers*

First published in Australia in 2009
by HarperCollins*Publishers* Australia Pty Limited
ABN 36 009 913 517
harpercollins.com.au

HarperCollins*Publishers*
25 Ryde Road, Pymble, Sydney, NSW 2073, Australia
31 View Road, Glenfield, Auckland 0627, New Zealand
A 53, Sector 57, Noida, UP, India
77–85 Fulham Palace Road, London, W6 8JB, United Kingdom
2 Bloor Street East, 20th floor, Toronto, Ontario M4W 1A8, Canada
10 East 53rd Street, New York NY 10022, USA

National Library of Australia Cataloguing-in-Publication data:

Glover, Richard.
    The mud house / Richard Glover.
    ISBN: 978 0 7322 9029 0.
    Glover, Richard.
    Clark, Philip.
    Friendship.
    Earth houses – New South Wales – Taralga.
302.34

Cover concept by Natalie Winter; illustrations by Sharyn Raggett
Author picture by David Anderson
Internal design by Alicia Freile
Typeset in 11.5/16pt HoeflerText Roman by Kirby Jones
Printed and bound in Australia by Griffin Press
70gsm Bulky Book Ivory used by HarperCollins*Publishers* is a natural, recyclable product
made from wood grown in sustainable forests. The manufacturing processes conform to
the environmental regulations in the country of origin, New Zealand.

5 4 3 2 1   09 10 11 12

FOR PHILIP

This book contains really stupid advice.
Please don't follow it.

ONE

It was 1983. I was in Canberra for the weekend and my friend Philip was serving a meal. He'd bought himself a pasta machine and was creating spaghetti for four. The kitchen was in disarray. He'd used every pan in the house and splashed every wall with tomato sauce. As the mixture bubbled away, he discussed his latest passion. He'd discovered that certain wineries sold port in bulk — packaged in 12-litre plastic bladders which you then bottled yourself.

Philip rummaged around in his pantry then turned to face me, holding aloft two schooners of port. 'Here — have some,' he exclaimed, pushing the glass into my hand.

I took the glass and studied it against the light. 'I didn't know port was meant to have a head,' I said.

'Take no notice,' replied Phil. 'It's fresh from the bladder.'

I hoped he meant a bladder of the plastic kind. I took a sip.

'Tastes good,' I lied.

He leant down conspiratorially. 'Actually, it's a headache in a bottle. But at 20 cents a glass ...'

Philip served up the meal and I helped him carry the bowls into the living room. Our girlfriends were sitting at the table, waiting to be fed. Gillian, Phil's partner of a few years, studied history; Debra, my more recent girlfriend, was trying to make it as a playwright. The two liked nothing better than raving to each other about the books they were reading.

Philip swung back to the kitchen and returned with two more schooners, placing them with a flourish in front of the women.

Debra lifted her glass and held it against the light. 'I didn't know port was meant to have a head,' she said.

'It's fresh from the bladder,' Phil repeated, with the tone of a proud sommelier.

We got stuck into the food and drink, and Philip and I joined the discussion. Neither of us had read the novel in question but, in this group, total ignorance did not appear a barrier to expressing a firm opinion. We drained our port schooners and Phil poured another round.

Phil had not only made the meal, he'd also made the table at which we sat. It was beautifully constructed, from Huon pine, with a pale, silky surface. I was hardly a craftsman but even I could comprehend the skill involved in its dovetail joints and bevelled edges and I complimented Philip on his achievement. With his second port in hand, Phil enthused about the table, the art of woodwork and how he loved the feeling of making something with his hands.

He put on an LP — one of the stack of Bob Dylan records he played almost constantly — and the four of us danced to the music. The women were wearing jeans and Indian cotton tops. I found them both spectacularly attractive. I wanted us all to be friends forever.

Philip and I decanted another bottle of port and managed to spill a good measure over our feet. 'That's for later,' I confided. 'I'll be able to suck that out of my boot on the way home.'

I went back to dancing while Philip took a breather, sitting back at his handmade table, running his fingers idly over the surface. 'One day,' he mused, 'I'd like to build something bigger. A lot bigger. No, a LOT bigger.' He wrapped his knuckles hard against the wood. 'Like a house,' he added. 'We could just buy a block of land, you know, the four of us, and have a go.'

I laughed. Well, snorted really. The girls laughed. The idea was absurd. We all ignored it and kept dancing.

←

Six months later I was in a car, sitting beside Philip, bumping down a dirt track somewhere in the bush north of Sydney. We were trying to buy a block of rural land on which we could build a house from scratch, using our own labour. It was an absurd proposition. Even as I navigated down the bush track, I couldn't believe I had agreed to something so unlikely. I didn't have the skills to change a light bulb. I had trouble differentiating a chisel from a screwdriver. I had never used a circular saw. There was no way I could take part in building a house.

Philip was my best friend, but we were a study in opposites. He was stocky, with a barrel chest, dark skin and curly, black hair. At school he'd been a champion weightlifter, and his body was still compact and muscly. He was a dedicated law student, but read fiction voraciously — setting himself the challenge of reading every new Australian novel. He had a certainty about him, a self-confidence that I envied.

I was paler, thinner, more neurotic, my shoulders drooping apologetically forward like a letter 'r'. I thought of myself as a bit frayed, as if I could unravel at any time. I found it hard to be in the moment; always feeling as if I was watching myself, and passing judgement on my own behaviour. It was as if my brain was not in my own body but perpetually hovering above it — a mordant, black-hearted crow.

I'd never been a practical, hands-on sort of guy; more the wan, bookish type. From the age of 12 or 13, my main hobby had been the local youth theatre club. Much of my adolescence had been spent lying on my back pretending I was a melting ice-cream, or running in circles, my arms flapping, embodying the spirit of the North Wind. (You'd have been impressed; I was the spitting image.)

At school they had tried, and failed, to make a man of me. Forced into the rugby union team, the coach would scream from the sidelines: 'Glover, pick up the ball, run with it.'

'Can't, sir,' I'd yell back. 'Might get hurt, sir.'

At athletics they'd try to get me to jog with the others around the field. 'Well,' I'd say, 'since you'll all be back so soon, would you mind terribly if I just waited here?'

I'd even scribbled 'ballet' on my school sports form — taking advantage of a loophole which allowed boys to fulfil their sport commitments with out-of-school activities. The school authorities had in mind such manly pursuits as yachting, fencing and mountaineering, yet, for two terms, they let me off twice a week to attend the Belconnen Ballet Centre, where I produced some of the worst performances ever seen in the history of modern dance.

'It is good to have a boy in the class,' the teacher had observed, contemplating her troupe of 29 girls and one boy. 'But it would be marvellous if you were strong enough to lift your partner more than an inch off the ground.'

At age 15, I even got into a serious schoolyard fight. Of course, it was over a novel. As I sat on the grass reading during lunch hour, some scoundrel stomped on my book — a treasured copy of PG Wodehouse's *Right Ho, Jeeves*. 'Dash it all, man,' I protested, jumping to my feet. 'You can't step on another chap's book.' In my choice of words, I may have been overly influenced by my reading material; the phrase 'dash it all' was not particularly common in the mid-'70s Australian schoolyard. It certainly brought a look of festive merriment into the eyes of the lad who, thus encouraged, was about to become my assailant.

If I'd been reading Ernest Hemingway or Dashiell Hammett I may have won the bloody, scrappy fight that followed; instead, I had to take comfort that my reputation as a bookish weirdo had been confirmed.

The school doubled its efforts to make a man of me, forcing me to do a course in woodwork. In this class, tasks were allotted according to the skill level of the student. While my schoolmates built tongue-and-groove scale models of the Eiffel Tower, I busied myself with the 'breadboard' — the optimistic name for the rectangle of wood given to the slow boys.

'It's not that difficult, Glover.'

'Alas, sir, I find it so.'

After a year of breadboard studies, they moved me on to more complex tasks, such as the pencil box with the slide-on lid. Here at least there was room to move. If the lid wouldn't fit into the groove first time, you could make the observation: 'It will loosen up over time.' Then, when the teacher wasn't looking, you could approach it with a hammer and attempt to make it see reason.

The woodwork problem, in retrospect, was more than simple incompetence, laziness and a pretentious desire to be different, although they all contributed their share. Like a handful of my peers, I had trouble identifying with the sort of masculinity that seemed be on offer. Being a 'normal bloke' in mid-'70s Australia didn't seem a matter of choosing from a rich smorgasbord of possibilities; it felt like being strapped tight into a straitjacket. There was a checklist of required behaviour, tastes, enthusiasms, with little room for error or even for some minor eccentricities. On offer seemed to be a take-it-or-leave-it package deal — which included an obsession with sport and beer drinking and a negative attitude to both women and book learning.

Being a normal bloke didn't seem to deliver much to an inward-looking, book-obsessed boy like me. And so, increasingly, I threw myself into the world of youth theatre, which at least seemed to bring a broader definition of being a man. Plus, as a bonus, lots of girls.

Youth theatre in the '70s was dominated by ideas of improvisation, method acting and the acquisition of as much body hair as possible. Thick matted hair was everywhere — on chins, legs and chests. The men were even worse. Yes, an old joke, but by 1974 the whole troupe looked like Cousin It from *The Addams Family*. We'd head off together for rehearsal weekends on the south coast, where the combination of long hair and physical intimacy provided a breeding ground for pubic lice that has never been bettered.

Just occasionally we'd take a break from the cultivation of body hair and stage an actual play, but it was always about a subject like rape in war, or the general subjugation of women. For a boy going through a problematic adolescence, this provoked a thoughtfulness about masculinity which I hope has stayed with me, but perhaps too large a helping of gender self-doubt.

I remember one day lending a hand to move equipment ready for our performance of *Palach*, a cheery piece about a student activist who self-immolated when the Soviets invaded Czechoslovakia. I was standing with another 17-year-old boy, both of us idly scratching ourselves in response to the latest lice infestation, when one of the girls asked us to help lift a rostrum into place: 'Could you men lift it over there?' was all she said, her voice upbeat and kindly. But we both heard the word 'men' as an insult, a slap across the face, as if she'd called us rapists. We remained where we were and, sensing she'd said the wrong thing, she corrected herself: 'Felix, Richard, would you mind?' It was a measure, mostly, of my own bubbling insanity over gender, but also of the youth theatre world of the time.

Which brings us back to the subject of building skills and my complete lack of them. It all went a bit deeper, you understand, than just not knowing which end of the hammer to hold.

←

So there I was, 26 years old, my neuroses still intact, sitting in a car with Philip, trying to find a block of land suitable for building a house. How exactly had *that* happened?

By this time Debra and I had moved to Sydney, but on each occasion we returned to Canberra for a visit, Philip would idly mention his idea of building a house. Each time, the snorting and laughter seemed less intense. Then, one weekend, Debra wondered aloud, 'So if we did buy a block of land, how much do you think it would cost?'

This question, once put, was hard to ignore. Building the house together would maintain our friendship with Philip and Gillian, despite our life in a new city. Who knew, it might also allow me a way to feel better about being a man; of resolving this shadow from adolescence.

We grabbed a newspaper from the stack in their laundry — one with Saturday classifieds. We checked out the list under the heading 'Rural Land'. There were quite a few blocks for around $25,000 to $30,000. A lot of money, of course, but between four of us ...

Philip decanted another offering from his 'headache in a bottle', and by the end of the night we'd talked ourselves into it, with quite a lot of help from the bladder of port. What was I thinking, signing up to this sort of macho undertaking? Simple intoxication must bear most of the responsibility. Slurring wildly, we'd taken a sacred pledge. We'd all start to collect our share of the money — seeing how much we could earn or borrow. And I would start ringing estate agents and circling ads.

Ads like the one in my hand just a few weeks later, as I sat in the car next to Philip, bumping down a steep track, heading into the valley and bickering about whether he had missed the turnoff. The vehicle was Philip's ancient

Toyota, its suspension old and loose, a settee on wheels. The ad which I'd circled promised a block of land fronting onto Wheeny Creek, near Colo in the lower Blue Mountains. It was 50 acres, with good access. The price tag was $32,000. That was more than we could afford, but you never knew.

'This can't be right,' Philip complained, as the road got rougher and rougher. I checked the ad again but there it was: 'great access'.

Philip was not happy. 'There's virtually no road. I thought you asked about the access.'

'I did. The real estate agent said you could drive a Rolls-Royce down here.'

'Right,' grumbled Phil, 'there just wouldn't be much of the Rolls left by the time you reached the bottom.'

It was the fourth block we had visited. None had been suitable. First up had been the place with 'lovely water views', which turned out to be a marshy flood plain, the farmer sinking in the mud just as he began speaking about what a great building site it would make. Second up, the incredibly cheap land north of Sydney — just $30,000 for around 200 acres. 'What's it like?' we asked. 'Well, I probably should mention the gravel mine next door,' admitted the estate agent. 'But if you ever need cheap gravel it'll be a great advantage. The trucks go right past your gate.'

Then there was the block near Goulburn, infested with blackberry bushes and lantana — weeds so noxious you could cop a council fine if you left them uncontrolled.

You could see the farmer appraising the two city slickers and thinking he may as well try it on. 'It's a beautiful block,' he said, circling his arm to indicate the vista. 'You'll love picking the blackberries for a picnic — and the lantana is lovely in the spring.'

Maybe this Wheeny Creek land would be fourth time lucky. Philip was still nosing the car forward, yet with every metre the path seemed to deteriorate. It was a convict-built road, constructed from large squares of sandstone, the blocks of which had shifted over time so that now big fissures ran across the surface.

Declaring defeat, Philip parked the car beside the track and we continued on foot. Within 100 metres, what road there was pretty much disappeared and we found ourselves jumping over metre-wide crevices.

'So,' challenged Phil, 'how's your Rolls-Royce going?'

At the bottom of the so-called access we reached the creek. The block, we realised, was on the other side and we needed to wade through the water to get there. It was also clearly a flood plain. And thoroughly infested with bamboo and lantana. It was a measure of our desperation that we found ourselves seriously considering it.

'You could bring materials in by four-wheel drive,' Phil fantasised, staring at the creek, 'and then rig up some sort of flying fox to get them across.'

'And,' I added, 'we could build the house on stilts to avoid the worst of the floods.'

We walked back up to the car trying to motivate ourselves into this ridiculous, useless block of land; a block with zero access and multiple building problems. Only by the time we reached the car did some measure of sanity reassert itself. We'd need to look further.

←

While we searched for land, the house began to take shape, at least on paper. We began construction in our minds — letting the project dig its claws into us. We envisaged a two-storey building arranged around a giant fireplace. Or a house of stone nestled into a hillside. Or a giant cubby lifted high on tree poles. Philip produced pencils and pads. It was that glorious time when all is possibility; where you sketch and talk and argue; the house growing and changing shape — sometimes single storey, sometimes double; a few words or a line of pencil enough to add a whole wing.

As we dreamt about the house, I was becoming more enthusiastic, actively shrugging away my lack of building ability. What did it matter that I knew nothing about construction? Maybe I could be the eager assistant, while Philip did the proper work. Maybe I could teach myself the skills I lacked. Maybe this stuff wasn't as hard as it seemed.

I started bringing home books from the library: architecture books, hippy building magazines, and technical pamphlets from the CSIRO's building research centre. A few months before, my bedside reading had consisted of modish novels and back copies of *Theatre*

Australia. Now I found myself sitting up late, thumbing through a book about septic tank installation.

'Fascinating,' I mumbled to myself in bed.

'What?' asked Debra, returning her book to the stack of Iris Murdoch novels which she was doggedly reading back-to-back.

'People in Britain are experimenting with systems of open ponds, in which the sewage enters at one end and pretty clean water comes out the other. It's like an above-ground septic system.'

Debra peered over and allowed me to trace how the solid faecal matter passed through the system of reeds and ponds. I enjoyed the feeling of her soft breast leaning against me as I showed her the progress of the floating English turds.

'It *is* fascinating,' she said, and appeared to mean it.

We'd met at university, Debra and I. She was staging a uni production of Joe Orton's *What the Butler Saw* and I'd wandered in offering to help paint the sets. When I first met her, people regarded her as formidable. She had a sharp wit and passionate views. She bubbled with ideas. Later, I would walk over to her table at the university refectory, and there'd be a bit of chuckling among my old schoolmates, a sort of 'Ohh, brave man, brave man'. One of the sporty jocks from school even nicknamed her 'the Panzer tank'. But I never found her formidable; I found her thrilling and forthright. I particularly loved the way she lacked 'enigma', that popular quality of the time; she was always keen to express exactly what she thought.

Right now she loved the idea of the bush block. Or maybe more accurately she loved what it was already giving to me. I still hadn't handled a hammer, but at least I now wanted to give it a try. Maybe it would also give me a stillness, a centre, that I'd lacked up to now. Plus the chance to test out my long-held theory that you could learn anything from a book.

If only we could find the right block of land.

TWO

Another rainy weekend in Canberra. As usual, Debra and Gillian had colonised the lounge room, talking intensely. Philip and I were in the kitchen. He'd just purchased a hippy magazine called *Grass Roots*, and had it open on his kitchen table. Inside was an article about building with mudbricks. I flipped through the pages. Making mudbricks looked like incredibly hard work.

'I don't think we should get into this,' I bleated. 'We'd kill ourselves just making the bricks. We'd never get started on the house.'

Philip stood up and started pacing around the table. 'Don't make your mind up so fast. Imagine this — with mudbrick you have a building that is made out of the very earth it stands on; it's like it has grown out of the ground — like some sort of, um, growth. Or, um, tree.'

He was in a poetic mood, even if words were failing

him now and then. He had, it's true, taken delivery of another large bladder of port and was subjecting it to a fairly rigorous round of taste tests.

Phil leant against the fridge, gesturing at me with the port schooner in his hand. 'Think of the bog man in a Seamus Heaney poem. You build a mudbrick house and it would be like a prehistoric bog man clambering out and, um, well standing there.'

He flashed me a look of delight, convinced I'd be won over by this insane port-soaked vision.

I started to say something but Phil was lost to his mania. He marched around the table, bending down towards the floor and whooshing his hands through the air as if to summon a building into existence. 'The very ground rises up and becomes the form of the building. It's like a cathedral drawn from the earth.'

He stumbled around like this for a while, bending towards the floor, fluttering his hands down then pulling them upwards. I hadn't seen a dance routine this ridiculous since my own work — aged 15 — at the Belconnen Ballet Centre. I cradled my face in my hands and waited for the one-man dance troupe to finish. Finally he sat down.

'There is another thing,' he observed, suddenly matter-of-fact. 'The stuff is free. Once we buy the land we'll have no money left. This way we can get started as soon as we have the block.'

Actually, it wasn't a bad point. Once I was on my second schooner of port I began to see the force of his argument.

A few days later, back in Sydney, I started my research. In Australia, the popularity of mudbrick had waxed and waned. The early settlers had used wattle and daub — a method in which you build a framework of tree branches then pack mud into the gaps to make a wall. Mudbrick had been popular in the bush in the 19th century, especially for building barns or stables, but had lost out to the ease of corrugated-iron sheeting, hammered onto a frame of saplings. In the 1930s it enjoyed a revival at Montsalvat, an artists' colony just outside Melbourne, but by then knowledge about making mudbricks was so scarce, the leader of the colony, Justus Jorgensen, had to rely largely on a description he found in the work of Roman historian Pliny. By the early '80s, when we were hatching our plans, mudbrick construction was considered an eccentric choice.

'What happens when they get wet?' Debra asked as I thumbed through my stack of reference books. 'Don't you just end up with a big pile of mud?'

Fair question, but the bricks, I learnt, are amazingly resilient. Even sitting out in a field, a brick — once it's been dried in the sun — can hold its shape for a couple of months. Placed in a building, with a roof and good eaves, it is incredibly durable: even when heavy rain comes in at an angle and lashes the walls, it just hits the bricks and runs off. This has surprised everyone — right back to Pliny, who, in AD77, expressed amazement that mudbricks seemed stronger than quarried stone.

Following Jorgensen's lead, I bought a copy of Pliny's *Natural History* and read his vivid description of Hannibal's watchtowers in Spain — still standing after 300 years:

> Are there not walls made from earth in Africa
> and Spain... and do they not last for ages,
> undamaged by rains, winds, fires; and are they
> not more sturdy than any quarried stone?
> Even now Spain looks upon the watchtowers
> of Hannibal and the earthen turrets located
> on the mountain ridges. Such is the natural
> substance of earthen sod suitable for
> the fortifications of our camps and for the
> embankments against the flood of rivers.

I consulted Debra and then rang Phil.

'I hate to say it, but you were right. I think we should go with the mudbrick.'

'It will save a lot of time,' he chided sweetly, 'once you realise I'm always right. From now on let's take that as a given.'

So mudbricks it would be. Phil and I both studied up on the detail. Chimneys, we learnt, needed to be made out of conventional fired bricks, since the column sticks through the roof and is exposed directly to rain. And you need a few layers of normal fired brick on top of your footings, just to get the mudbricks away from the ground, so that heavy rain doesn't splash upwards and weaken the wall.

The bricks, we also noted, are large — each one the size and thickness of a big-city phone book, and weighing about 15 kilos. And environmentally they are very superior: they are made on site, so there's no transportation involved; they require no energy, other than a few days drying out in the sun; and they create a brilliantly well-insulated house — cool in the summer and warm in the winter. And, as Philip had implied, the houses are beautiful, the earth-coloured bricks naturally matching their environment.

Most soil is suitable for making the bricks, we discovered, but not all. So as we searched for a block we had something new to add to the list of requirements. Not only did we need land that was lantana-free, with easy access, at a cheap price, the soil had to have appropriate properties for making mudbricks. Whatever that meant.

←

After more months of failed expeditions, we focused on the mountainous country west of Mittagong — halfway between Sydney and Canberra. I found an ad for a block that at least sounded good:

> MITTAGONG/Wombeyan Caves.
> 64ha (160 ac) approx 10 ac level, balance
> undulating, spring fed dam, creek, power
> and building permission, views, car access.
> Price $29,000.

I rang Phil and read him the ad. I loved the romantic sound of the creek and the spring-fed dam. Philip heard nothing but the phrase 'car access'. After our terrible experience at Wheeny Creek he was suspicious.

'I'll bring my Rolls-Royce,' is all he said.

I checked out a rural newspaper — the *Land* — and found another block on the same road. It sounded even better:

> MITTAGONG/Martins Pass. 280 ha (700
> acres) river frontage, road frontage, views,
> building approval. Price $30,000.

I couldn't believe it was so cheap. I rang the estate agent to get more details. 'What's it like?' I asked.

'Mainly vertical,' was the terse reply. I gathered it had been on the books for years. The estate agent had been worn down over time to an astonishing new policy called 'honesty'.

The four of us met in Mittagong to inspect both blocks. Philip and Gillian jumped into our car and we headed due west, through the mountains. The road started out well enough but then the asphalt turned to dirt and the road narrowed. It snaked down towards the Wollondilly River in a series of hairpin bends. On one side was a sheer drop — a cliff looking over the Burragorang Valley far below. On the other side, a mountainous slope, bristling with rocks. Philip started humming the theme from *Deliverance*.

The road was difficult but the landscape was amazing. It was as if someone had taken a sheet of paper and scrunched it into a loose ball. There was hardly any flat country; it was all folded in on itself, with dramatic views from the ridge tops, and deep gullies cut by creeks.

After 30 or 40 minutes we found the turnoff to the first block — the 700 acres. The estate agent was right. It was largely vertical. We left the car on the road and scrambled down. We found ourselves surfing on the side of a mountain, teetering on a loose scree of granite. There wasn't enough flat land to lay out a Lilo, never mind build a house.

As we climbed back up towards the road, Debra, panting with excursion, imagined aloud another real estate ad for the place: 'Suit family of llamas.'

'Or,' Gillian added, 'those with an interest in abseiling.'

'I'd like you to also note,' wheezed Philip, gasping for air, 'the total lack of vehicular access.' Ever since Wheeny Creek the man had become obsessed.

We jumped back in the car and drove onwards to the second block. The road, remarkably, became even worse. There were now regular signposts saying, 'Beware Falling Rocks', sometimes featuring a picture of a car about to be crushed. Sitting behind the wheel I wondered what I was meant to do if a boulder came hurtling towards us.

I noticed another regular sign — 'Sound Horn at Blind Curves' — necessary since the hairpin bends prevented you from seeing a car coming the other way.

The two warning signs fought for my attention. I tried to pick an optimum speed: slow enough that I could stop before hitting an oncoming car; fast enough to minimise our chances of being crushed in the next landslide. At least there were laughs: every single 'Sound Horn' sign had been vandalised by locals to read 'Sound Horny at Blind Corners'. The four of us chanted orgasmically on every turn: 'Oh, yeah, baby.'

We crossed the river and headed towards the second block. The road went on and on and on, snaking upwards.

'Where is this block?' moaned Philip. 'Melbourne?'

With every turn you'd think you'd made it to the top and then another climb presented itself, as if the road was made of stretchy material and just as you were about to arrive someone stretched it longer. Finally we came to a clearing and spotted the turnoff, an even narrower road, out along the ridge top. Up here, there were actual patches of flatness. We started to become mildly hopeful.

Parking at the farm gate, we found the owner waiting for us. He was about 30 years old, with an open, tanned face. He'd been running sheep on the place but had decided it wasn't worth the effort, so he'd bought a block of better country down on the flat, over the other side towards Taralga. He was honest about the limitations of this

block in terms of grazing. There was an invasive weed — serrated tussock — and most of the block was pretty steep.

'On the other hand ...' he said and pointed to the view. We looked out over the rough, crumpled country we'd just driven through.

He left us to ramble about. The four of us walked down towards the 'spring fed dam', as featured in the advertisement. We didn't talk much; we were probably waiting for the inevitable unpleasant surprise. Soon, we'd stumble over the asbestos mine, get stuck in the forest of prickly pear, or peer over the rise and spot the motocross course next door. We walked down the path and emerged looking out over the paddock with the dam. It was bordered by forest on two sides. The day was bright and warm, and the gum trees shimmered in the heat, their leaves looking silver as they reflected the sun. Sunlight glinted on the small dam. As we headed on towards it, we noted a level patch of ground — perfect for making mudbricks. I caught Debra and Gillian sharing a smile.

We hiked back along the track to where we first met the farmer, through a stand of mountain ash and yellow box. There we found a large clearing with the remnants of an old shearers' hut on it. It would make an excellent house site, quite close to the road. I could hear Philip muttering to himself, 'Look at the access.'

The shearers' hut was long abandoned; it had collapsed and its tin roof and slab walls lay on the ground. A couple of horses grazed nearby and Debra paused, tempting one of them to come nearer. The horse ambled over and allowed her to stroke its muzzle. Well, there was her vote. And Phil? He was already in, won over by the short, flatish track that linked the house site to the road.

I walked up to the remains of the hut and examined one of the wooden slabs. It was hand-cut; there were axe marks where someone had shaped the wood. I wondered how long it had been there and the answer came almost instantly. Turning the slab over, I could see fragments of newspaper stuck to the wood. Someone had wallpapered the inside of the building with sheets of the *Goulburn Post* to stop the wind whistling through the cracks. You could still read the date — May 27, 1940 — and the two front-page headlines: 'BARRICADE IN FRANCE' and 'RIVER POLLUTION ALLEGED'. The slab hut could be older, of course, but it had been here for at least 40 years.

There was no lantana, no blackberry. The house site had been untouched by bushfire for at least a generation. And there was a good spot nearby to make mudbricks. It was also spectacularly beautiful, in a lean, hard sort of way. Up here, you could sense the bony skeleton of the land just under the surface. The place had an austerity about it. It was the sort of land that Judith Wright wrote about in 'South of My Days' — '... bony slopes wincing under the winter ... clean, lean, hungry country'.

Back on the ridge top, looking down on the house site, the sky was huge. You felt on top of everything. From the car, I fetched a topographic map. A few kilometres away there was an old placename that

*Phil stands in front of the old collapsed hut on the
day we decided to buy the land.*

Debra stroking one of Peter Chalker's horses.

summed up the landscape: Top of the World. I read out the other placenames scattered close by: Tumbling Creek, The Devil's Stairs, Lord's Mountain, Dead Man's Creek, Rack-a-Rock Glen and the Pass of Killiecrankie. We were less than three hours' drive from Sydney, but it felt like wilderness.

We'd found the perfect block.

We drove back to Mittagong to the estate agent. Already the road felt adventurous rather than dangerous. We arranged to pay a 10 percent deposit — scribbling out a series of cheques that added up to an incredible $2900. We were landowners. As we split up to drive back home, I wondered about the time ahead — and the point at which Philip would first hand me a hammer. The main question: would I know how to use it?

THREE

We were sitting around the campfire while Debra prepared her butterflied Kashmiri lamb. We'd owned the block for five weeks and already were acting like rural aristocracy. Philip had even brought a bottle of red wine. He'd discovered a bottle-it-yourself winery that sold shiraz in 12-litre bladders. It was more expensive than the port but produced a less intense headache in the morning. I was worried about him. At 25 cents a glass for grog, he was turning into a yuppie.

We sat on slabs of wood, souvenired from the collapsed shearers' hut, then propped on milk crates to make a couple of rough benches. A freezing wind whipped over the ridge. If you built up the fire, you could achieve a situation in which your front side would develop third-degree burns while your back half froze with hypothermia. We didn't allow these conditions to dent our enthusiasm.

'Isn't this terrific?' Gillian gushed, her teeth chattering slightly.

'Yeah, it's great,' I replied, my eyes stinging from the smoke. 'Can't wait for dinner.'

For some reason, we believed campfire cooking had to be as complicated as possible. Back home we'd have a meat pie from the local shop, but up here things were meant to be special. The week before, Philip had done a whole fish in Thai spices. It was quite badly burnt and eaten in a gale-force wind while perched on a log.

'Just delicious,' we'd chorus as we chewed through the charred corpse.

In preceding weeks, Gillian had created a pile of blackened cheese atop carbonised vegetables (quite disgusting), while I'd had a go at lamb-and-leek stew in the camp oven (not so much cooking; more an exercise in animal sacrifice).

Now it was Debra's turn to try and tame the coals. She was sitting at a rickety fold-up picnic table, with a gas light for illumination, mixing together yoghurt and spices. Philip was on his third glass of 25-cent shiraz, and was expounding his theory of water collection.

'You know what?' he exclaimed. 'We should make sure the roof is really steeply pitched. That way, we'll collect more rain for the rainwater tank.'

Even I knew this theory made no sense. 'It doesn't matter how steep the roof is,' I replied. 'What matters is the size of the house. Put a flat roof on a house of 12 squares and you'll collect the same amount of rain as if you built a pitched roof. It all depends on the amount of sky you've got covered.'

Philip looked at me with disbelief. He restated his argument several times, his certainty increasing with each rendition.

Debra paused in her yoghurt mixing and came in on my side. 'I guess,' she reasoned, 'if you had high winds, then a tall roof might capture more of the sideways rain, but the effect would be marginal. It's all down to the square-meterage of sky that has tin beneath it collecting the rain.'

Philip was baffled by our unwillingness to see reason. He grabbed the lids from two eskies and made a scale model of a pitched roof. 'Look at all that tin,' he insisted indicating the lids, 'and imagine all the water it will collect.' He then created a flatter roof using only one lid. 'See,' he crowed, triumphant. 'Less roof, therefore less rain will be collected.'

Debra put down her yoghurt and marched over. 'Forget the lids. Just concentrate on the esky itself.' She mimed rain falling out of the sky, wiggling her fingers and sashaying from side to side. It looked like the sort of rain dance they do on *Play School*. Or my own appearance as the North Wind with Canberra Youth Theatre.

The argument went on and on. Gillian, who was at first on our side, was starting to waver. Phil was so certain of himself that it was hard for anyone to maintain a contrary position. I started doubting myself, EVEN THOUGH I KNEW HE WAS WRONG. Luckily, I had a distraction. I busied myself with the fire, whacking down the grill and trying to reduce the conflagration from 'nuclear holocaust' to mere 'fire storm'. Debra was still doing her Esky Dance, but Philip would brook no opposition. He had the mania of the true believer.

'I'll just be a second,' he shouted and rushed off into the darkness, up towards the old shearers' hut. He appeared to be in search of props to illustrate his theory.

While he was gone I placed the yoghurt-drenched lamb on the barbecue. It instantly burst into flame. Using tongs I pulled aside some of the bigger pieces of wood, in the process burning my right hand and singeing off both eyebrows. There was now a sharply acrid smell in the air — an intoxicating mix of incinerated human hair and charred dairy product. I dulled the pain with a large draught of Philip's 25-cent shiraz.

Phil then re-emerged from the dark, dragging a huge sheet of rusty tin. Clearly he thought us too stupid to understand a scale model so he was going for something closer to life size. He was starting to build the house right here, in the dark, by the fire. In a moment he'd fetch buckets of water and measuring devices.

Luckily, I needed his help to get the ruined meat off the barbecue. Together, we lifted the blackened sacrifice from its altar. 'How about,' I said, 'we agree to research the rainwater issue when we get back to town.'

'Too right,' said Philip as we carried the meat to the table. 'I've got a mate in the Department of Science. And I'm sure he's going to agree with me.'

It was my first inkling that Philip's certainty and

optimism sometimes needed a little tempering; that maybe I'd be called upon to be more than just his labourer. I had no practical skills whatsoever, but in the face of Phil's boundless self-confidence, my nail-biting, stomach-churning, self-defeating, black-crow anxiety might finally prove an asset.

We squeezed around the little table and started prodding at the mix of charcoal and meat on our plates. The food was entirely cold, having been exposed to the wind for as much as two seconds. After a couple of mouthfuls of frozen carbonised lamb, Philip held up a piece on his fork, showing it off to the group as if it were a thing worthy of study.

He turned to Debra. 'Delicious,' he beamed. 'Food tastes especially good up here.'

'It's brilliant,' I agreed, and — as the gale-force winds picked up — we all toasted our good fortune.

←

It was the morning after the Conflagration of the Kashmiri Lamb and we were expecting a visitor. Our friend Michael had promised to give us his caravan — a small, old-fashioned model in the shape of a baked bean. He no longer had anywhere to park it.

'It can sleep four,' he told me when he made the offer. I'd only seen it from the outside, parked in his street in Sydney, but even this modest claim seemed unlikely. The thing was tiny.

Still, the campsite could do with an extra amenity, however meagre. At this point our settlement largely consisted of two tents, which would be erected by the headlights of the cars when we arrived, usually late on a Friday night. Putting up the tents in darkness and buffeting winds was not pleasant work. There were a number of poles, seemingly identical, which had to be inserted in a set order. Inevitably, I always left a crucial piece behind. It was particularly tricky putting in the tent pegs, as there was always a large rock just under the dirt wherever one chose to hammer. Banging away at midnight, trying to chance upon a gap in the rocks, I'd wonder how exactly we were going to make mudbricks on a block so seemingly devoid of dirt.

Our campsite also had a shower. Well, 'shower' may be too grand a term. It was a canvas bag, which you filled with hot water and hoisted onto a tree branch. You then stripped off and stood naked under the bag, the trickle of warmed water proving no match for the cyclonic winds which would spring up the instant you removed your clothing. Considering myself very witty, I gave the bag a name: 'Denis the camp shower'.

Michael arrived at lunchtime on Saturday, towing the old van, ignoring all the signs declaring the road 'unsuitable for caravans'. I thought of Philip as having a zest for life but Michael was even sunnier. He pulsed with optimism and energy. Jumping out of the car, he bounded around the block like a dog who'd been shut up indoors. Michael jogged up to the collapsed hut,

Debra and me camping on the block in 1984.

praised the shower and paid his respects to the wonderful view, all within 30 seconds of driving up. Then he paused and clapped his hands together. 'Time for the grand tour.' He then flung open the door of the van and waved us in.

'You'll love it. You'll be amazed,' he enthused, as if we were about to be treated to a tour of the Palace of Versailles.

We squeezed into the tiny, ancient van, ducking our heads to get in the door. We shuffled even tighter so Michael could squeeze in. Yes, it could sleep four but only as part of a *Guinness Book of Records* attempt.

Michael loved the van. He'd been around Australia in it. Through his eyes, this towable baked-bean transporter was a magical place. 'Nearly everything does two things,' he said, his voice high with wonder. 'This is a bench top,' he announced, hammering it with his knuckles. He paused until we all nodded our assent that, yes, it was indeed a bench top. 'But it is also a stove.' With a magician's flourish he lifted a section of bench top to reveal a tiny two-ring gas cooker. He pointed out the other facilities. 'The sink is hidden here, there's a water pump there, a fridge behind that panel, and then the *pièce de résistance*: this may look like a breakfast nook, but that is only by day. At night it converts into a ...'

Michael started to convert the nook into a bed, butting us occasionally with bits of wood until, finally, we were forced to watch from outside as he removed the various cushions, heaved the table upwards and out, dismantled its legs, then reinstated the table as the bed base and made a mattress from the cushions.

Five minutes later, red-faced and sweating, he popped his head perkily out the door. '*Voilà!*' he proclaimed. 'Simple as that. A comfortable double bed erected' — he let out a pant of effort — 'in seconds.'

←

The caravan was a great addition to the block, but it was hardly an alternative to a house. We would have to get on with the building. Step one, of course, was to make the mudbricks. Here, like Justus Jorgensen at Montsalvat, we had to take note of the Roman historian Pliny, and the warning he made in his *Natural History*: mudbricks are great but you need the right soil.

Back at home I fetched my copy of Pliny and read it to Philip over the phone. 'Pliny says that the bricks should be made from a chalky clay and white or red soil.'

'Really?' said Phil.

'Yeah,' I said. 'He also says that you can use a bit of sandy soil, but only if it's masculine sand.'

There was a pause on the other end of the phone. 'I hadn't been aware, up to now, that sand had a gender.'

'It's not my idea,' I protested. 'I'm just reading out the standard Oxford translation.'

'It probably,' reasoned Phil, 'means sand that is coarse and unrefined.'

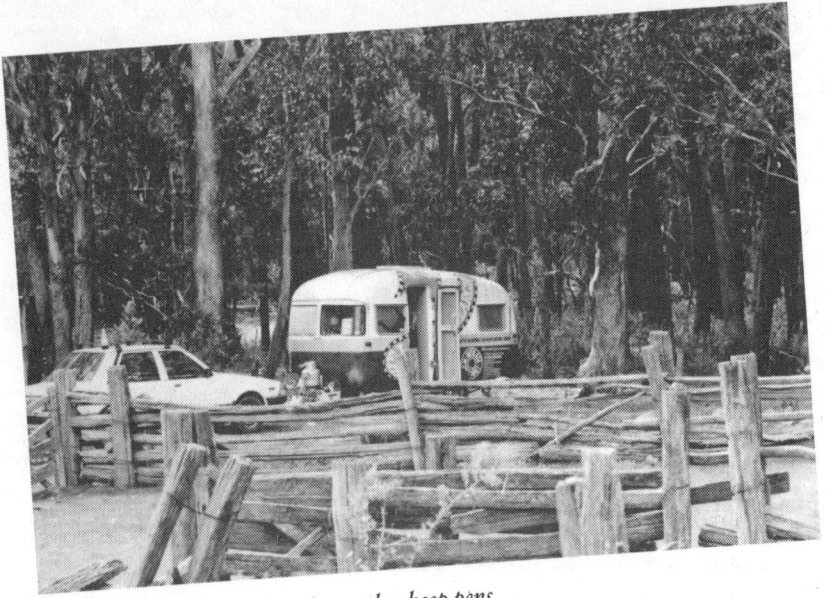

The baked-bean van stationed near the sheep pens.

I laughed, thinking he'd made a joke, but Phil said, 'Actually I'm serious. That's probably what it means.'

'I guess so, anyway ...' I returned to reading out the Pliny. 'He says the worst thing is bricks which are made from soil that is gravelly or, even worse, stony.'

I paused for a moment before stating the obvious: 'That's like a description of our block.'

Philip cleared his throat. 'Maybe you shouldn't be relying on a book published 2000 years ago. Who knows, you might find there's been something published a bit more recently.'

It was a reasonable point. I pledged to visit the library.

Our phone call was about to end when Philip added an afterthought. 'Oh, I asked my friend in the Department of Science about the roof and how much rain it might collect. He, um, basically agreed with you guys. It's the footprint of the house that determines the catchment, not the pitch of the roof.'

'Really?' I said.

'Still,' he added, 'I think a steep roof would look better, don't you?'

A few weekends later we were back at the land, standing down in the dam paddock in the morning sun. There was one way to find out whether your soil was up to the job: you make a proto brick for testing and send it to the brick testing laboratory. There it would be sprayed with high pressure hoses to see if it held its shape. At the end of the process the laboratory would send a report — either giving the go-ahead or announcing that 'your soil is not suitable'. It was our first make or break moment.

To get us started, Philip had made a timber mould. It looked like a desk drawer with the bottom cut out and handles on both ends. We set about mixing our first load of mud.

First there was the matter of collecting a pile of dirt. I grabbed the mattock to start digging, swinging it hard into the earth. It hurtled down towards the ground then bounced. My Herculean swing left hardly a dent. The other three laughed. I tried again, heaving it harder this time, but again it bounced off — scattering enough dirt to reveal the tight layer of small stones just below the surface. The soil was like a Christmas cake of crushed rock.

Philip, rolling his eyes, took the mattock from my hand. 'You need to put a bit of force into it,' he insisted, swinging the tool through the air with a weightlifter's oomph of effort. To my immense pleasure it hit the ground and sprang back. Again, hardly a dent. We all laughed harder. Maybe this was why the farmer seemed so cheerful when he sold us the block: the only crop you could grow here was pebbles.

We attacked the ground once more, stabbing at it with picks, shovels and mattocks. After a while, we'd hacked it sufficiently to accumulate a small mound of soil and stone. We separated them into two piles.

'Note the way,' sighed Philip, 'the pile of stones is twice the size of the pile of dirt.'

We shovelled the hard-won dirt into a wheelbarrow and added a few strands of straw to help bind the mixture. As instructed by the more recent books, we sprinkled in a tiny quantity of cement — more benediction than real ingredient. Last came a bucket or two of water, carried up from the dam. We took turns in mixing it, working the mud with a spade until it had the right consistency — wet enough to fill the mould but dry enough to hold its shape once the mould was removed.

'It's like making a cake batter,' Gillian observed as she worked. 'You just flip it and pummel it until it's smooth.'

One of our wooden moulds.

Finally Philip heaved a shovel load of mud into the mould. He sank down on his haunches and plunged his hands into the thick mixture, pushing it down into the corners of the wooden rectangle. He added some more mud to fill the mould completely and then splashed some water on the top. Using a length of timber, he carefully smoothed it off, gave the mould a wriggle, and then pulled it upwards.

'*Voilà*!' he declared, standing to admire his work. A perfect mudbrick was left sitting on the ground: our first. We gave a cheer.

It had taken us about two hours to make this first brick. We made another 10 just for the practice. To build the house, we needed 3500 of them. At this rate, the place would take slightly longer to build than the cathedral at Chartres. I remembered a phrase I'd read in *Walden* — Henry David Thoreau's book about living and building in the woods. He reckoned the longer a place took to build, the longer it would last. On that reckoning ours would last centuries.

Philip put one of the bricks into his car, ready to send it to the testing station as soon as it was completely dry. 'We'll have to see,' he said. 'Maybe it will fail the test.'

I found myself thinking: we can only hope. That way we could give up on the mudbricks, build the bugger out of Besser brick, and cut about five years off our workload.

FOUR

Our block was long and thin — a strip of land stretching back from the small dirt road. There was a flat bit near the road, then it crumpled into a series of steep gorges and bony ridges, full of mountain ash and yellow box. Walking from one end to the other took about 40 minutes — down into one valley, up a steep ridge, down into another valley, and up to a final ridge.

At the bottom of both valleys there were tiny creeks. Both surged into action after rain, then just as quickly emptied out again. For most of the year both creeks were reduced to a broken necklace of ponds. On the top of the ridge, marking the back boundary, was a collapsed fence from decades before: a strand of rusty wire snaking between old strainer posts.

The place was full of such signs of the past; remnants of people who'd had a go and then moved on. We dug into the ground near our planned house site and came across a pair of old boots and an old cordial bottle: 'Brooke's Fruit Squashes — C.M. Brooke and Sons' Property — Absolutely the best.' We uncovered a couple of rusty rabbit traps: the steel jaws lolling open as if they were still ready to bite, even though the spring had long ago rusted away. There was also an ancient sheep pen, built from hand-cut timber, slowly falling to pieces. If you dug where there had once been a gate, you'd find an old bottle buried upside down, the punt of the bottle providing a pivot point.

I tried to imagine what life was like for whoever lived here, up on this distant mountain top in the '20s or '30s, clearing the land by hand, bringing in supplies by bullock train from Taralga, about 40 kilometres away. I wondered how they managed to get the wool to market, all the way down to Goulburn on the flat. And how they could make a living on these small blocks of rough country.

The land we'd bought was about 850 metres above sea level, high by Australian standards. Seen on a map, it sat in a circle of mountains, like the centre of its own kingdom. It was part of the Great Dividing Range, the spine of hills that runs along the east coast of Australia, in most places a couple of hundred kilometres inland from the coast. On one side, the flat coastal strip; on the other, the dryer inland plains. Fingers of national park reached up the hillsides — bushwalking through the country you might cross into the Blue Mountains National Park, the Wollondilly River Nature Reserve or, a bit further north, the Kanangra-Boyd National Park. Down in the valley, a half-hour hike away, were the Wombeyan Caves, a knot of startling limestone caverns.

European settlers came in the 1820s — initially to the country around Goulburn and Taralga, and then into the surrounding hills. The first Europeans reached the caves in 1828, searching out grazing land for the wool pioneer John Macarthur. As early as 1865, Charles Chalker was appointed permanent caretaker of the caves and visitors started to arrive.

In the 1880s and 1890s the Wombeyan district seemed to be really hopping. A guesthouse was built at the caves; famous visitors such as the painter Conrad Martens arrived to paint scenes. Taralga, meanwhile, was booming   locals building distinctive houses and churches from the local grey-blue stone. In 1900 the road to Mittagong was completed: the crowning glory a section of tunnel cut through solid rock. It was celebrated with a grand opening, with politicians from Sydney, dressed in their finery, toasting the decades of good fortune that lay ahead. There was even talk of a rail service following the course of the road — bringing tourists to the caves and opening up the sheep country further west.

Somehow, though, the boom never quite arrived in the way expected by the early settlers. The road through the mountains has stayed much the same as on that opening day. Jenolan Caves took over from Wombeyan as the more popular destination — helped by a sealed road from Sydney. The guesthouse at Wombeyan Caves burnt down in the 1930s and was never rebuilt. And the population of Taralga started to drop. The town had streets full of empty lots — space left for buildings which were never built.

In countries such as America, the early pioneers were nearly always proved right: settlements got going and became bigger by the year. If only you'd bought land in Chicago in the 1840s, or in Los Angeles in the 1920s. Not in this country: Australia is full of places where optimism was defeated. There are success stories, of course, but the nation's rural population has been in decline since the 1920s. Towns — especially small towns — get smaller each year and sometimes disappear. Maps are dotted with these extinguished settlements — on a driving holiday in the Aussie bush, people plan a rest stop in the largish-looking dot on the map only to arrive and find it's nothing but a single broken-down barn.

There's something quite elegiac about these vanished places and the small towns that struggle on. I like them, just as I like battered furniture, worn-out briefcases and old, abandoned train stations in the bush. I like their dogged survivor spirit.

Up here on our mountain top the serious farmers had mostly moved on too — the blocks too small, the land too unforgiving. Amid the beauty there was a sense of defeat in the air, especially in the wild hills — as if this country has often lifted people's hopes only to smash them down.

I wondered whether we'd be next.

←

Philip and I decided to install a gate into the dam paddock: our first bit of real handiwork. We found some instructions in a book and set about following them. Up early one Saturday morning we removed a section of the fence, cut two strainer posts from the bush using an axe, dug two holes, then started to reconnect the old wire. By about 11am, we had the job pretty much finished. That was when Peter Stiff came driving past.

We already knew Peter fairly well. He was about five years younger than us — maybe 22 or 23 — and worked on Tallygang, the one serious farm left in this part of the mountains. Peter had returned to the district after a few years rodeo riding. Ask him how many bones he's broken and he'd proudly run through the litany — 'Here, here, here, here and here,' he'd say, pointing out each busted part of his body in turn. He'd also supply his own name — Stiff — with a note of challenge, as if daring you to make a joke about it.

Peter hopped out of his battered ute and came striding towards us. He was gangly and plain-spoken, with an old bush hat pulled down low.

'G'day boys,' he said. 'Been doing a bit of fencing?'

This, you understand, was spoken with considerable irony. He stood, legs apart, arms folded, and gave our workmanship an appraising look. His eyes swivelled over the narrow strainer post and the too-shallow hole into which it was propped. He noted the spindly brace sitting ready for installation.

He paused for effect. 'Well, if I was going to build a gate, I wouldn't start that way.'

Peter then offered his immediate assistance. We accepted, not quite understanding the extent of the offer.

'Yeah, well first of all, I'd pull that strainer post out, just throw it away, and we'll start the whole thing from scratch.'

Philip stared mutely at the interloper. It had taken us three hours of gut-busting effort to get to this point. Philip looked like he was about to mount a protest but I hopped in first. Resistance, I'd decided, was futile.

'Well,' I agreed, 'if you say so, Peter.'

Peter nodded grimly. 'It's just nowhere near big enough, that strainer post of yours. It won't last. You'll be back here in five or ten years putting in a new one.'

Philip again looked like he was about to say something — something like: 'Well, five or ten years doesn't sound so bad.'

Again I got in quick. 'Give us orders, Peter.'

Peter strode back to his ute, fetched his chainsaw and cut into a nearby tree. It fell with a roar. He trimmed a massive strainer post, twice the size of ours, and deftly removed the bark. 'You two boys grab the post and just whack it on the hole.' He stood with his chainsaw dangling in one hand and watched as Philip and I approached the beast.

'It's, ah, quite large,' Philip observed.

'Ah, yeah, it'll do the job,' drawled Peter, striving for an Academy Award in the category of 'most laconic bushie'.

Phil and I positioned ourselves one on each end. We bent down and threaded our hands beneath the log. Phil did the countdown: 'One ... two ... three ... up.' We heaved upwards. The thing didn't shift at all. The log was oblivious of our efforts.

Not so Peter. A tickle of a smile played about his lips. 'Let me help you there boys.' He then strode over and bent down over one end of the log. Inserting his fingers under the fallen trunk, he lifted his end then suggested we might join forces in lifting the other end.

It is rare in life that, just after 11.30 on a Saturday morning, you find yourself able to predict the topic of conversation that night at the Taralga Hotel, its ebb and flow, the faces leaning in with merriment and the howls of laughter as Peter reaches the climax of his tale about the two city boys unable to shift the 'really quite small' log he'd just cut for their gatepost.

Still, we had learnt how to build a proper gate. And commenced our role as comedians for the district.

←

The next weekend we headed down to the Taralga pub ourselves. If nothing else, we could entertain the locals first hand. We walked in to find four young blokes lined up at the bar. I'd noticed their vehicles on the way in. It was pretty obvious they were pig hunters. They had two battered farm utes, each with a big cage mounted on the tray. Inside both cages were a couple of mangy-looking dogs. They were piggers of the sort that didn't use guns. They used dogs, poor ravaged animals who were trained to hunt the pig down, latch onto its ear and hold it to the ground. At this point, the pigger would move in with a knife and plunge it into the pig's heart.

As I waited at the bar to order our drinks and food, I asked one of them about their plans. He was around my age, 26 or so, with a raw-boned face, a wispy beard, and a beanie pulled right down to his eyebrows.

'We're just having a few beers and then we'll head up to the scrub and get a few pigs.'

For people involved in such a brutal sport, the piggers were pretty friendly, but I felt sorry for their injured dogs. The animals were often missing ears, or had noticeable gouges across their chests. I'd spotted some wearing protective leather breastplates, like doggy centurions. You could learn good lessons about masculinity in this part of the world but there were some models I was not so keen to follow.

'What do you do with the pigs once you get them?' I asked.

'We're planning to buy a refrigerated truck. Then we can sell the pigs to Germany. Over there they call it wild boar. There's a lot of money to be had. A lot of money.'

The bloke with the wispy beard pressed his lips together and nodded his head in a knowing way. His three companions looked up from their beers and nodded in agreement, like three canny entrepreneurs who'd just been given an angle on the world price of gold.

'Apparently it's easy money,' the first bloke said, and — as if on the promise of these riches — bought all his mates another round of beer.

Our hamburgers arrived and Phil and I went into the back room to eat. Inside was an old pool table, a framed photo of the local footy team and a blackboard with the latest footy results.

'There are only three teams in the local competition,' Phil noted as he walked past. 'You'd have a fair chance of making the semis.'

A couple of blokes were playing a desultory game of pool. They greeted us with a tiny nod of recognition. I'd met them a few weeks before, coming up the road near our place in a small truck. One guy was very large but sounded a bit dim; the other was a ferrety little bloke, but smart. They reminded me of the characters in *Of Mice and Men*, Lennie and George. They'd previously told me they had permission to collect firewood from some place down the end of the road. As I finished off my burger, I asked casually about the property and who it was that owned it. They seemed uncertain about the details. I got the impression it might be wiser not to press the point.

Phil and I had another couple of beers and left them to their game. The pub emptied out and we took our turn playing pool. Phil found the one Bob Dylan track on the jukebox and played it three times in a row. Finally, just before closing time, the pub received another visitor. A bloke stumbled in and straight away I could tell he was a local from up in the hills near our place. I knew this because he was wearing pink shoes.

Up near our block, the council had ordered everyone to control the spread of serrated tussock by spraying it with poison. When you sprayed, you added red dye to the herbicide so you could see which areas had been done. The mist of dyed poison would end up on everything, especially your footwear. As a result, the hills were full of big tough blokes with fuck-off beards, sporting bright pink footwear. This newcomer to the pub was no different. He pretty much summed up the Wombeyan look: wild hair, grease-stained work pants, a flannelette shirt and luminous pink boots.

He wasn't in a happy mood. He'd checked his water tank earlier in the day only to find it empty. 'Some mongrel is stealing my water.'

'You don't think you just left the tap on?' I asked.

'No way. It's happened twice this year. Someone knows I'm not there Saturdays so the mongrel is coming in and pumping the stuff out.'

This struck me as unlikely but what would I know. The guy ordered his beer and stood there sullenly drinking, enjoying his status as a repeat victim of crime. He sighed in a world-weary fashion and stared down at his bright pink boots.

'I'm going to catch him,' he said, finally looking up with a half-smile. The boots, it seemed, had given him an idea.

'Next time the tank's full, I'll put dye in the water. Then when the water's nicked I'll come down here and if that bastard has been using my water to wash his clothes, I'll know straight away. He'll have pink clothes, the mongrel.'

I looked at him and wondered what to say. Pouring red toxic dye into your own water supply certainly represented a plan. I just didn't know whether it was a good one. I imagined the scene in the Taralga Hotel in a week or two. Some poor innocent from the Canberra Public Service would turn up on Sunday drive dressed in his natty new pink shirt, just purchased from Country Road. The instant he walked in, the cry would go up.

'There he is fellas, the mongrel water thief of Wombeyan.'

The guy would then be beaten senseless, all the time proclaiming his innocence and trying to convince the locals that new season pink was merely his favourite colour.

'It might work,' I said meekly.

'Mate,' the bloke replied, 'there are a lot of morons in these hills.'

←

We'd finished the gate and were now ready for a bigger job. Our shearers' hut was flat on the ground but the building materials were still usable — especially the hardwood slabs, which had been split by hand from the box trees nearby. They weren't pieces of timber; more like tidied-up logs, trimmed of their curved edges. When they built the hut, the slabs would have been placed in vertically, the end of each slab tapered so it could fit into a groove in the rough frame.

'We need a shed to keep the tools in,' Phil said. 'This timber's fine. We should recycle.'

We began collecting the old slabs, pulling them free from the collapsed building.

'I'll be engineer for the project,' I said as I dragged a slab of wood towards the sheep yards.

'How will you achieve that?' inquired Philip. 'Do you plan to flip through Pliny until you come across a section marked "shed design"?'

I ignored him. In fact, I'd purchased a comparatively recent building guide. *The Reader's Digest Do-It-Yourself Manual* was a book from just a few decades past — full of 1960s-style home beautification projects — purchased for $2 at the Mittagong St Vincent de Paul. With its help I'd be able to knock-up a tiled breakfast nook with built-in bench seats. Or a Pebblecrete patio with built-in barbecue. Or a Spanish-style cocktail bar. Sure, there was no specific mention of a bush toolshed built from recycled hardwood slabs but I could improvise.

I dropped the slab on the site of the new toolshed and headed back up the hill for the next one.

'Actually I've got a copy of *The Reader's Digest Do-It-Yourself Manual*,' I bragged.

'Great news,' said Phil. 'We'll be able to build a Pebblecrete patio with built-in barbecue. Or a tiled breakfast nook with built-in bench seats. Or maybe a Spanish cocktail bar.'

It seemed he was already familiar with the publication in question.

We spent a few weekends assembling materials and then both took a week off work to head up to the block and tackle the construction. We dug four post holes then used a chainsaw to cut some saplings. I'd never used a chainsaw before, and was terrified I'd cut off one of my legs. I'd specially chosen a machine rated by the Australian Consumers' Association as the safest on the market, and was now discovering the reason for its rating: it had a lot of trouble cutting wood, never mind your leg. Its action was like that of a beaver, slowly chewing through the fibre. As I gnawed at some saplings, Philip stacked more of the old slabs ready for reuse.

After an hour of effort, and much cursing of the Australian Consumers' Association, I was able to present four wooden poles — each trimmed to a bit over two metres. Aside from the ill-fated gate, it was my first handyman job since the pencil-box-with-slide-on-lid in school woodwork. The results were not pretty. I'd hacked at the trees with a chainsaw, axe and even a sledgehammer. The poles were now covered in welts and bruises, like a small boy's legs after a rough game of soccer. The ends were mangled, as if they'd been chewed by sharks. Philip helped me lift them into the pre-dug holes. They stuck upwards at weird angles, wonkily marking the corners of the shed-to-be.

'Actually,' I observed, 'that's a pretty good job.'

'Well, no one's going to be looking at them,' Phil conceded.

Phil then took over the chainsaw and did a rather quicker and neater job cutting four more saplings. We used them to connect the tops of the poles, creating a rough cube, with timber battens across the top for added strength.

Philip was all for hammering the roof straight onto this structure but I had my doubts. With my two books spread out, I insisted we add some support struts at each corner.

'They are called "braces",' I announced to Philip.

'You don't really need them,' he contended. Several times.

'I think we do,' I insisted. Several times.

Finally Phil agreed to look at one of the illustrations in my handyman book. A pause and then a concession speech: 'Well, I guess you could do it that way.'

It was my first experience of a dialogue we were to have many times over the next 20 years. Phil's practical skills were amazing, but that didn't mean he was a perfect decision-maker.

With the frame complete — including braces — we started to lift the old slabs into place. Damn! They were too short to go horizontally, but also too short to fill the space vertically. In a stroke of pure brilliance, we decided we'd build a rock wall up to knee level, top it off with a wooden beam, and install the slabs vertically on top of

The shed takes shape.

that. Suddenly they became a perfect fit. Such creative problem solving, of course, would not be open to anyone who had the foggiest what they were doing.

We began work early each day and worked until nightfall. Then there'd be a quick visit with Denis the camp shower, and then down to the campfire for some incinerated meat. Sitting with a beer by the fire, I had a flickering realisation that we might prove good team-mates, Philip and I. We had different temperaments and different levels of skill at building, but we were both serious workaholics. We loved throwing ourselves into the task; seeing how much we could achieve by the end of each day.

The rest of the crew, Debra, Gillian and our friend Belinda, arrived on the weekend to find the shed almost completed. They ignored the strange mix of materials that made up the wall; it did, after all, seem to be holding together. With the full team, we set about finishing the job. After decades out in the weather, the hardwood slabs were like steel. With no power on site, we had to use a hand-drill before attempting to drive in a nail.

We found an old door on the block, and worked that into the design, and managed to reuse the old tin from the shearers' hut for the roof — lining up the sheets in order to conceal the bits that were entirely rusted away.

The three women declared they were in charge of the front wall of the shed — hammering on some overlapping boards, also souvenired from the shearers' hut. They called it 'the girls' wall'.

By the end of the weekend the job was finished: a lockable shed that looked as if it had been there for decades. If anyone passed by they would surely date it to the 1930s and might even wonder about this traditional half-timbered building style, in which a rock-wall base gave way to slabs. I was unaccountably proud of the whole thing. My first building.

As dusk came on the Sunday evening, Philip and I shared a beer, contemplating our achievement. 'It's a bit rough,' I said, overcome by my usual doubt.

'Well,' said Philip, 'it's not meant to be the ceiling of the Sistine Chapel.'

It was a phrase that was to become our catch-cry — the answer to all the imperfections and disasters to come.

FIVE

As the shed progressed, I was intrigued by the recycled wooden slabs. Old axe marks were still visible, especially at the ends, where the slabs had been bevelled. There I was hammering nails into those bevelled ends cut by an axeman many decades before. Who was he? When did he do this work?

In this district, there was a chance I could find out. Up here, the same surnames kept cropping up: families who had arrived in the 1830s or the 1840s and never left. The local phone book, if you had one for this small patch, would be dominated by just four names — Chalker, Fleming, Lang and Cree. Many of the caves at Wombeyan had been mapped by Charles Chalker, the first superintendent of the site; one of his relatives, Michael Chalker, was running the place now. It was from Michael's cousin, Peter Chalker, that we had bought our block. Peter himself, when I asked about this family history, put it this way: 'In the old days, if you kicked a tussock up there, a Lang or a Chalker would run out of it.'

These were the real locals, but there was also some new blood. One newcomer was Bob Packham, the bloke who owned Tallygang. He'd only been here for 20 years. Bob looked the part of the gnarled old grazier, yet his story was more complicated. His father had been a farmer, but Bob had studied law and run a successful practice in Canberra with Lionel Bowen, later attorney-general in the Whitlam government. He'd bought the land in the '60s, tired of the law, and then moved into farming full time. After a few years at Wombeyan, he'd turned into a local — happily damning the lawyers and politicians of Canberra in the aggrieved tone of the true bushie. We thought he was fabulous.

I decided to ask Bob about the history of the area, wandering over to his place with a notebook in hand. I found him in his shed, tinkering with an old farm utility. He looked up and smiled. 'Damn thing's buggered.'

Like most bushies Bob took delight in adversity. For those living on the land in Australia, it's the best way to be. As I was already discovering, the bushie who delights in adversity can find himself enveloped in constant waves of joy.

'No choice but to fix it,' Bob grumbled as he prodded at the ute with a spanner. 'There's no money in wool.'

He stood up and propped his boot against the running board. Naturally the boot was bright pink. Life up here was like a weird production of *Priscilla, Queen of the Desert* in which the costume department had failed to supply anything but the footwear. Bob rubbed an oily hand on his ripped workpants.

'You can't fathom the way those idiots are running the wool business. They have baffled themselves with bullshit.' Bob had a booming voice that suited these sorts of phrases.

He was happy to talk about the landscape — the elevation and the solitude. 'It's great country for wool; you don't want lush country for wool; you need high, dry country, sparse country.' He also explained the name Tallygang — how, in the early days before proper fences, sheep would stray onto neighbouring blocks and then be brought together for an annual 'tallying', in which the strays would be swapped.

Bob was totally smitten with his wife, Joan, an elegant and whip-smart woman, who also did a killer line in gem scones. He hollered towards the house, demanding she bring him the car keys so he could try to start the motor.

'Where have you hidden the keys, Joan?' he boomed. He was so clearly in love with her he couldn't help but smile when he used her name.

And then, *sotto voce*, to me: 'You know, I'm thinking of starting a training school for wives. I think I'd get a lot of takers.'

I asked Bob about the old huts which were dotted around the place. I'd noticed our old hut was only one of many. Debra and I would be out bushwalking 30 minutes from the road, and we'd come across a collapsed hut. Same hand-bevelled slabs as our place; same collapsed tin roof and ruined rock chimney. Why had they been built in such profusion and who had lived in their tiny rooms?

As he waited for Joan to bring the keys, Bob explained the rules of what was called 'free selection'. 'In the old days you could claim 40 acres from the government and pay just £1 an acre. But you had to prove that piece of land was home to someone. So they'd send poor old granny out to live in some hut, and they might take her out a bucket of water every couple of weeks just to make sure she's not dead, and that way they could claim they were improving the land.'

Joan turned up with the keys and patted Bob on the head as if he were a wayward schoolboy.

Was there, I asked, a particular granny this happened to? Bob couldn't be sure; he'd just heard about the practice. I should talk to Ken Fleming.

Bob hopped into the ute and turned the key. The engine sprang into life. 'Bugger me,' he said looking up in astonishment at Joan and me. 'I fixed it.'

←—

Ken Fleming was already a fixture in our lives. He worked with Bob on Tallygang, and would always stop at our place on his way past, fascinated by the idea of using mudbrick to build. At one stage he did a two-day course in it, just so he could understand what we were up to.

Ken was also the district's amateur historian. He had his own place down near Taralga, with two or three sheds overflowing with historical memorabilia and old farm machinery. He and his wife, Joyce, even offered tours to passing motorists.

I visited him in his lair, again with notebook in hand. It turned out he knew plenty about the history of our block, right back to when it was first cleared.

'A relative of mine did the clearing work,' he said as soon as I asked. 'Actually, I've got the receipt and the contract.' He talked as if the work had been done the week before.

'When would that have been, Ken?'

'Can't quite remember. But it would be some time around 1921.'

As he searched for the paperwork, Ken explained how a block would be cleared ready for grazing. First the owner would ringbark most of the big trees — cutting a strip of bark from right around the trunk so the tree could no longer pump nutrients down to the roots. The tree would eventually die, but the crucial bit was preventing new trees growing up in its place — chopping out any new seedlings before they could get established.

Ken emerged from a low cupboard waving the handwritten contract. The sheet of paper carried the date April 1921. It was a contract between the then owner, Michael Chalker (of course it was a Chalker), and a local contractor, WJ Fleming (a distant cousin of Ken's). It called for William Fleming to 'scrub my paddock'. The handwritten contract then detailed the work involved: Fleming agreed 'to knock off all suckers and to pull up or knock out all seedlings over one foot high for the sum of £40 (forty pounds)'. There was a payment schedule of £15 on 2 May, and another of £15 on 1 June, 'providing I have sufficient work done', with the balance on completion.

Ken also had a photo of our hut when it was standing. Oh, and a wooden mallet that was found atop one of the rafters. He handed it to me — a rough chunk of hardwood fashioned into a primitive hammer. 'It's a rough old thing, but they would have used it to knock the slabs into place.'

And what about the granny that Bob had mentioned, the one sent to live in the old huts?

That would be Granny Lang. She was an amazing person. He also had a photo of her. Ken rattled over to the other end of the shed and returned bearing a photo of a stern, handsome woman of the old school. It was a copy, he said. I could keep it.

Ken and I stood together admiring the photo. 'You know she used to live alone up in those huts and walk all the way to Taralga — close to 40 kilometres — wearing a long black dress. She'd get supplies in town and then walk back, staying the night halfway. A very severe-looking woman but a great character.'

'Who did she stay with?'

'Oh, some Flemings.'

Of course.

I needed to know more about Granny Lang. She sounded like a good patron saint for a desperate bunch of mudbrick makers. I asked Ken how I could find out more. 'Well,' he said, 'you could talk to her grandson, Arthur Lang. He met her.'

History was reaching out and grabbing me. Around here, it sat close to the surface.

I gave Arthur a call. Arthur was in his late 80s, his voice still steady and his mind sharp. 'Granny Lang? Yes, I met her. When I was a young boy.'

He told me the story of his grandfather, Charles Lang, a Scot who married a woman 16 years his junior. Her name was Ann Burnett, the woman who was to become Granny Lang. They married in 1852 when she was 23 and he was 39, moving to Tallygang in the early 1880s, all their possessions pulled by bullocks. There Charles built a small bark-roofed hut for what became a family of eight children.

Arthur is downbeat about the land up on the mountain tops: 'If you wanted cheap country you had to take what was left.' They tried to graze sheep but there were so many rabbits that if you cracked a whip the whole hillside would move.

The real economy of the place involved shooting rabbits and living off the meat. Not surprisingly, the children moved on as soon as they were able, trying their luck elsewhere. By the time Charles died at the age of 84, there were only two grown-up children left, and they didn't stay long — selling off the property to fund a move to better lands. Widow Lang, at 68 years old, was left without a home.

As Arthur tells the story, it was his father, William Lang, who came to the rescue. 'When the other brothers sold up, Granny was left homeless. So my father selected a block in her name and built her a small house, down near Jocks Creek. As the years went on, my father selected some other blocks for her.'

Later, I went through the Department of Lands records and found a reference to that first block: an 80-acre rectangle with the words 'Ann Lang (Widow)' written in official copperplate, to indicate her ownership.

She died in May 1922 at the age of 93, after living as a widow for a quarter of a century. I wondered how often she'd been moved on, from hut to hut, on lonely hillsides. Was she being used by the family to accumulate its holdings or was she her own woman, busy building her own fortune?

From this distance it was hard to tell. Using the old Department of Lands maps I found at least five blocks which had been marked with her name in a process that went on over decades. In 1912 she was still busy — an annotation giving her permission to put a road through to one of her blocks.

I peered at Ken's photo of her. It showed a fabulously forbidding-looking woman — mouth turned downwards, looking to the side as if she had no desire to impress the camera. She has on a tight black hat and a black dress,

*Queen of the granny huts — Granny
Lang at her forbidding best.*

*The old shearers' hut, subject of a ridgy-didge Aussie bush yarn,
in its former glory.*

with a small lace kerchief tied at the neck. There's an admirable defiance about the tilt of the head.

I asked Arthur about the shearers' hut that had been on our block, but he'd run out of memories. He told me I should speak to Russell Chalker. The Chalkers were starting to blur and multiply in my mind, but I worked out that Russell was the son of Michael, the man who had signed the contract with WJ Fleming to 'scrub my paddock'.

I rang him in Taralga and he buzzed with pleasure when asked about the old block. He remembered camping in the hut in the late 1940s, when he was 15 or 16: 'The country lousy with rabbits.' He would ride his horse up to the block and then spend a week setting traps. He loved it. 'You didn't have a wireless, didn't have a telephone, no bugger to annoy you.' It was exactly what we were hoping for ourselves.

He recalled the old hut: 'A wooden slab floor, two small rooms — a bedroom and a kitchen, with a rock fireplace built into the side.' As he talked, I wondered if some of the items we'd dug up — a single old boot, a rabbit trap — belonged to Russell and dated from those teenage trips on horseback.

'Why did most of the farmers move on?' I asked.

Russell, along with everyone else I asked, gave the same answer: apart from the rabbits it was down to serrated tussock, cause of the ubiquitous pink shoes.

A weed from Peru, Chile, Uruguay and Argentina, it had arrived in Australia sometime around 1900, had infested the flat country by 1938, and by the 1950s had reached this part of the mountains. The tussock loved it up here, colonising paddocks that had already been partly destroyed by rabbits — the two imported species joining up to deliver the one-two knock-out blow. The tussock couldn't be eaten by sheep or cattle, and a dense infestation would reduce carrying capacity to almost nothing.

Russell let out a sigh. 'It was the ruination of that country.'

I asked him about the hut. Did he know who built it?

'Actually, I do,' he said, his voice brightening. 'It was built some time in the 1920s by two brothers who worked for my father, two old bachelors from Bannaby. Their names were Paddy and Jack O'Connor.'

It was they who had split the slabs which we were now busy recycling. According to Russell, they were paid £1 a week plus food.

'But that's not the best bit of the story,' crowed Russell. Down the phone line I heard a chuckle of laughter. I urged him on.

'It's probably just one of those stories.'

'Tell me.'

'Well, the story goes that Paddy and Jack were building the hut together. Paddy was working on the inside of the building, hammering the slabs into place. And Jack was on the outside, lifting the slabs into place. And they worked right around the building like this, forgetting that they hadn't put in a door. So when they finished, poor old Paddy was left inside, imprisoned, with no way out. He was belting on the wall, yelling, "Let me out, let me out."' Russell laughed.

'It's a great story,' I said.

'Well, it's certainly been told in our family quite a few times. About once a year for 50 years.'

I felt a rush of pride on behalf of our old hut. Not only had the bevelled wood survived to be reused in our shed, it was also the subject of a ridgy-didge tall-tale Aussie bush yarn.

In the space of a few days I'd learnt two things. The block had a rich history. And it probably wasn't much use for grazing.

What was it good for now? Well, possibly it was perfect for a crew of city slickers with something to prove — using inspiration from the resolute Granny Lang.

SIX

The sample mudbrick had been put through its paces. At the testing station in Sydney it had been sprayed with high pressure hoses and poked with sticks, as if it were some goblin or incubus. An envelope arrived with the results. I opened it nervously then rang Philip to tell him the news.

'The soil's OK. It's going to work.'

We now had to start making the bricks — about 3500 of them according to Philip's back-of-an-envelope calculation. Peter Stiff helped out with the Tallygang tractor, pushing up a big mound of dirt on the flat pad of land near the dam.

The four of us stood there watching him work.

'That's a fair pile of dirt he's pushing up,' whimpered Gillian.

Debra tried to reassure her. 'Remember it's mostly rock.'

'Oh,' bleated Gillian, 'that's alright then.'

Peter finished off and left us to it. 'I don't know how you're going to get all those rocks out of it,' he said, flashing a smile as he puttered away on the tractor. Peter believed we had rocks in our heads as well as in our soil.

'Good luck,' he hollered as he reached the gate, somehow conveying the message: 'Do call me for more assistance once you give up and decide to build using besser brick.'

We dug a pit the size of a deep bathtub, in which we could mix the soil and water. But first we had to separate the soil from all the rocks. We set about making a huge sieve from rough timber, one metre square, with chicken wire nailed across the bottom. We'd sieve out the rocks. How hard could it be?

We hammered a long piece of timber into each side of the sieve to create a pair of giant handles. Debra and Gillian took one end, Philip and I the other. We placed the contraption over the pit, then the four of us started shovelling it full of soil. Some of the dirt fell through straight away but most ended up sitting atop the wire in big damp clumps. We downed tools, picked up the sieve and attempted to shake the dirt through.

'How heavy is this bastard?' groaned Philip as we lifted.

We shook our arms and bodies, heaving the thing up and down and from side to side, like we were dancing a weird mudbrick watusi. Some more dirt trickled through but most of it just stayed there, rolling around on top of the wire. Finally we put the sieve down and leant over it, scrabbling at the wire with gloved hands, forcing the clumps, one by one, through the chicken wire.

'Laborious enough for you?' asked Philip.

'Both time-consuming and unpleasant,' Debra replied brightly.

The sieving was a lot of effort but the dirt that fell into the pit looked fantastic — light and aerated, like sifted flour. We added a small spadeful of cement to each pit load of mud, and a handful of straw to help bind the brick together. For a town-dweller straw was harder to come by than you'd think. I'd managed to pick up two bales that had been used as part of a shopping centre display. Two weeks before our hard work, those hay bales had been helping sell jeans in a country and western display; now they were being thrown in handfuls into the pit to make mudbricks.

Next we added the water. For each pit of dirt, you needed something like six big buckets of water, each one scooped from the dam and heaved up the hillside by one of us, a bucket in each hand. After three trips, I felt so much like a donkey I had an urge to bray.

Once all the ingredients were together in the pit we began the mixing. It was hard to know the best method. I started by standing astride the pit, heaving at the mixture with a hoe, pushing it backwards and forwards. The mud was incredibly heavy and viscous.

Debra watched me as I heaved at the thick porridge. 'You'll kill yourself doing it that way.'

Maybe she was right. I threw the hoe to one side and picked up a shovel, working it around the edges of the pit, lifting and turning each load. 'That doesn't look too good either,' she said.

My back was already hurting. I decided she was right. 'There must be a better way,' I said to no one in particular. Perhaps if I used a pick?

I chopped at the surface with a pick, trying to get the dry bits to mix with the wet bits. It didn't go particularly well. 'You don't look a happy man,' said Debra, alarmed at seeing the effect of real work on her ballet-dancing boyfriend.

The trick, I learnt over the coming months, was to develop a large repertoire of methods. That way, by the time you reached the end of the list, you would have forgotten the pain involved in method number one. Maybe that astride-the-pit-with-the-hoe-thing was worth another try?

Right now, though, I was making do with the pick, and after 10 more minutes of whingeing and mixing, a single pit's worth of mud was nearly ready. This was equal to about 40 bricks out of the 3500 required. As I mixed the load, Phil and I had the inevitable conversation:

Me (panting with exertion): 'How many bricks have you deducted to take account of the windows?'

Phil: 'A lot.'

Me (still panting): 'But maybe the windows should be bigger. A lot bigger. Big windows are very beautiful. Maybe we should have a building that is mostly glass,' —

my breathing getting even heavier — 'I don't think you can have too many windows in a building.'

Phil: 'Can you just get on with the mixing?'

In the end, Debra and Gillian came to the rescue. 'Give us a go,' offered Gillian.

'We'll show you how it's meant to be done,' agreed Debra.

The women spent a minute with the hoes, shovels and pickaxes and then decided the best method was to just get into the pit along with the mud. They stripped off most of their clothes, slipped on big gumboots and stepped into the mud, holding onto one edge as they worked their legs backwards through the mud, like a rugby back-rower in a scrum.

I could see Debra's leg muscles flex as she pushed hard against the mud. Philip and I stood back admiring the view: two young women, near naked, wrestling in mud, and yet producing a useful building material in the process. Life does not get much better.

The job completed, the women pulled themselves out of the sticky mixture, their bodies looking like they were made of clay. They ran down to the dam, jumped in and cleaned off. Then up the hill they came towards us, their figures glistening. Maybe mudbrick making had its benefits.

More importantly, the mud was now ready. We could make our first proper load of bricks. We set up the moulds on sheets of second-hand plywood, bought on the cheap from a recycling centre in Sydney.

I speared my spade into the mud mix, heaved it upwards, and carried the teetering load towards the mould.

'Delivery of brick-making materials. Ladies, gentlemen, please make way.'

I slopped the mix into the mould. Two shovel loads made a brick. Debra and Gillian pushed down on the mud, screed off the top surface and pulled the mould free. Phil washed out the mould and then set it up for the next load.

'Come on. More dirt,' he shouted, as I teetered up with another load. 'Mate, it's not a holiday camp.'

It took us about an hour and a half to empty the pit. We had made our first batch of 40 bricks.

We sat on our haunches admiring them, sitting out like loaves of bread baking in the sun. The day was incredibly hot — good weather to bake both the bricks and the brick makers. We were also covered from head to foot in dried mud and encircled by a cloud of blowflies. The fantasy mix of wet mud and sweat had attracted insects from all parts of the nation: it was so good they'd heard about it up in Darwin.

We swatted the pests away and tried to stand upright.

'I can't straighten my back,' moaned Debra.

'Me neither,' I whined, grimacing with pain.

This was one thing the books had failed to mention: every single step in the mudbrick process involved maximum pressure on the small of the back: digging the dirt, mixing it, shovelling it out again, making the bricks, moving the bricks, stacking the bricks.

'Suddenly it's obvious,' I announced. 'Mudbrick making was invented by chiropractors as a way of drumming up trade.'

The others whimpered their agreement. We were each bent double like 90-year-olds. Still, we had made 40 bricks. Which meant we'd have enough bricks for the house in just 350 hours of back-breaking, soul-destroying, fly-covered and mud-spattered hard labour.

'Remind me again,' I asked, 'why we didn't buy a kit home?'

'Because,' enthused Philip, 'this building is going to look terrific.' He articulated the last word syllable by syllable: 'terr-if-ic.'

Mudbricks provide an excellent building material, as well as continuing employment for the chiropractic industry.

After a few weeks the brick pile began to grow. Phil (left) seems to believe a beard will help, while the author shows off his ballet-dancer's legs.

By the end of that first day we had mixed and emptied two big pitfuls of mud and were left with precisely 72 bricks. (The pain involved in each brick allows for no rounding up or down of numbers.) The mud pit was surrounded by bricks, some sitting in groups of 10 or 12 on large sheets of ply; others sitting solo on smaller pieces of scrap. We left them drying overnight, and then — hopefully some time around noon the next day — we would be able to turn them onto their edges, exposing a fresh side to the air. Once they were dry enough we'd store them in stacks, covered over with tin to protect them from rain.

That night we celebrated. Sitting around the campfire we stared up at the house site, imagining the building was already there, the pale bricks picked out by the moonlight, all the while drinking enough red wine to dull the pain radiating in waves from our lower backs.

←

After months of talking and sketching, the plan for the house was finalised. A friendly architecture student had been bribed with food and grog to produce some drawings. The design saw a largish rectangular building

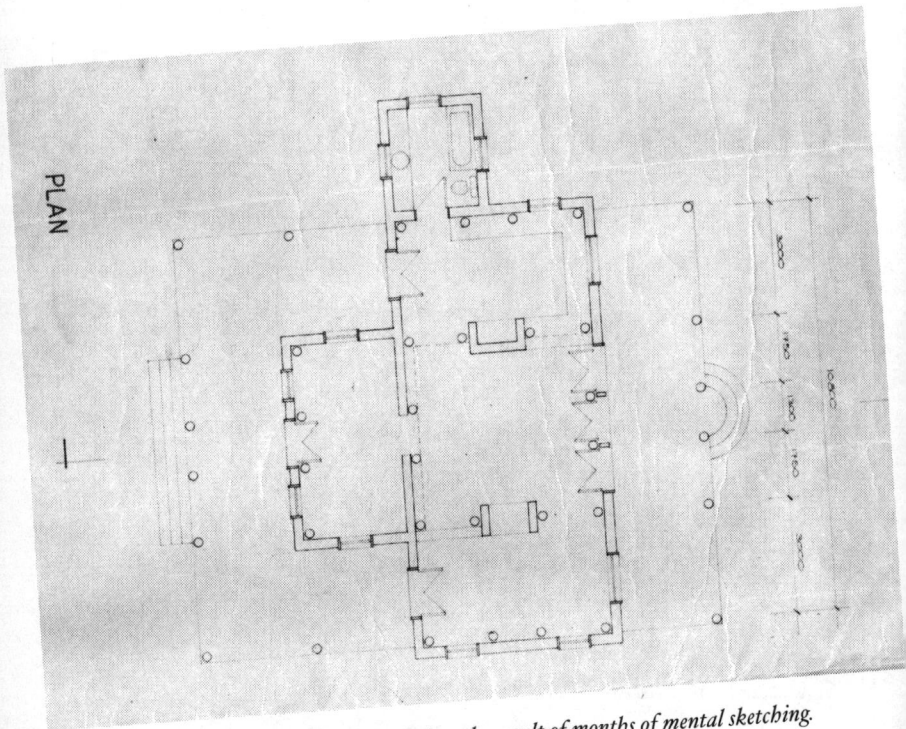

The grand plan, the result of months of mental sketching.

— 10 metres long and about six metres wide — with a kitchen down one end. Sticking out from the rectangle was a small bedroom on one side and a bathroom at the western end.

Thick poles cut from trees on our own block would hold up the roof. A steep staircase led to two loft bedrooms, built into the roof structure. The whole thing looked like a small church, with a large fireplace dominating the main space. It looked fantastic on the page. Now we had to summon the skills to make it look good in reality.

There's a limit to the number of mudbricks you can make in one go, mainly due to the intense band of pain that takes up residency in your lower back. We decided to spend some time marking out and digging the foundations — the trenches, about a metre deep, that marked the outside walls of the house.

Luckily for our backs there was some brainwork required before the digging could begin. We had the dimensions, of course, but needed to achieve a series of right angles. Debra and Philip believed this could be done using Pythagoras's theorem. If only they could remember what it was.

'I think it has something to do with the square of a triangle,' Debra said.

'Or the triangle of a hypotenuse,' said Philip.

'Or,' — Debra again — 'the square of the hypotenuse.'

They argued merrily over the details, sitting on an old log, gesticulating madly. Philip, the man so against taking advice from Pliny on the making of mudbricks, seemed happy to reach back the best part of three millennia for his own building tips.

A few hours passed until finally the two of them chanced on the right formula — *The square of the hypotenuse of a right-angled triangle is equal to the sum of the squares on the other two sides, as expressed in the equation $a^2 + b^2 = c^2$*. By calculating the squares of both front wall and side wall, they could determine the length of the hypotenuse, and thus create a neat right angle on the ground. That's what they claimed anyway. It was one of the few moments in my life where I'd seen the utility of paying attention in year 9 maths.

The foundations thus determined were marked using stringlines — two on each side — indicating where the trenches would have to be dug. Since I'd played no part in the brainwork, I took first turn on the pick, punishing the ground between the stringlines with a series of aggressive, ill-aimed strikes.

'Really, it won't take long. I'll just get stuck in.'

This, of course, was madness. There's a perfectly good machine designed for digging trenches. It's called a backhoe. Peter Stiff, who pushed up the soil for the mudbricks with his tractor, could have done the job at the same time. But we hadn't been that well organised.

And so I dug. And dug. And dug. The work went on for weeks. Each weekend, I'd dig a few hard-won metres of trench. The next weekend we'd return and find that it had rained, the sides had weakened, and the walls of the

7₈8/9 - DICK'S SUPERB TRENCH

The wrong method: Debra's caption for this picture was wildly optimistic. The trench never worked out.

Philip and I, in an act of insanity, use picks and shovels to dig away the hillside to fit the bathroom.

trench had collapsed. I'd dig it all out again. Forget Pliny and Pythagoras, the main ancient figure I was copying was Sisyphus.

The house site was fairly level, save for the area where the bathroom would be built. Here the land rose slightly, so we needed to carve out a bit of the slope. Again — insanely — we decided to do it with shovels and pickaxes — chewing away at the hillside over subsequent weekends. It was like trying to dig a swimming pool by hand — proof that we possessed, in equal measure, a gritty determination and a quite spectacularly low intelligence. I still have photographs from the time — Phil and I attacking a hillside with hand tools.

More enjoyable was the project of collecting the tree poles which would hold up the roof — 16 of them, each the diameter of a telegraph pole and about three metres in length. All had to be 'won' from the bush. Again, it was something we'd never done before. Mostly the technique was obvious enough — choose a good straight tree and chop it down, trying to ensure it didn't land on your head. But how did you get the bark off? Luckily, we'd had our experience building the gate with Peter Stiff.

As demonstrated by Peter, you needed to cut the log to the required size and then delicately run the chainsaw down the trunk lengthways, cutting a groove just to the depth of the bark. Then came the real trick. Using the back end of an axe, Peter had rained down blows on the log he used, basically giving it a rough massage. The aim was to break the fibres holding the bark in place, so it could be slipped off like a coat.

I enjoyed the way Debra threw herself into this work. She'd never been a lipstick-and-blusher kind of girl. Sometimes, going out on a special occasion, she'd stand uncomfortably in front of the mirror, gamely trying to apply some makeup, all the while muttering, 'I'm not a proper woman.' Up here, I loved watching her with the chainsaw, leaning into the tree with a fixed look of determination, enveloped in a cloud of sawdust and noise. Frankly, I found it pretty sexy. 'Timber!' she'd yell, and the carefully chosen pole would crash to the ground.

Winning poles from the bush. They're barkin'!

She'd then cut a groove in the bark and stand back while the rest of us employed the Peter Stiff method, beating at the bark like so many jungle drummers. After five minutes of beating, Debra would insert the axe head under the edge of the bark and prise it off — usually in one intact sheet. The pole would come out all glistening and pale, like a newborn child. We took to yelling, 'They're barkin',' to mark the moment at which the naked log emerged.

One by one we cut the logs and heaved them up to the house site, leaving them lying in rows propped off the ground on old pallets, so they could season before being used in the building.

The shed was finished; the foundations marked out; the first few loads of bricks were drying. I was even starting to enjoy the feeling of tools in my hand; when I handled a saw or a hammer it no longer felt like some strange object. We were also working so fast it looked as though we'd be able to start real building within a few months.

Just as long as our backs didn't give out first.

Debra and Philip admire tree poles now ready for building.

SEVEN

Mostly all four of us would head up to the land, but occasionally it was just Philip and me. Each time this happened I'd return home to be greeted with questions from Debra. 'What did you two talk about?'

'Nothing.'

'You've spent a whole week together. How can you have talked about nothing?'

The truth was we mostly abused each other. Get two Australian men together and they will express their love and affection by verbally attacking each other. A building project is the perfect opportunity. Your hands may be busy with a screwdriver but your mouth is free to describe the personality flaws and the physical defects of your most treasured friend. By the end of the first year of building, I was not only learning to use tools; I was also learning how to partake in this rich male tradition.

Whatever my doubts about masculinity, as conventionally rendered, I found that this was a game I loved playing.

Come closer and listen to Philip's worksite banter. According to his account I am ignorant, weak and gap-toothed. I also have long, gangling arms of the sort most commonly found on a gorilla.

He, on the other hand, is short. Really quite short. It's a fact I'd like to impress upon you.

We were building a bark hut, slung off the side of our toolshed. We planned to store the mudbricks in it. Philip stood on tippy-toes, trying to slip a piece of guttering into place. 'Here,' I said, 'why don't you let a man of decent height do that for you?'

'Fuck off,' said Philip.

'I just don't want you to have to stretch.'

'Well, why don't you use your knuckle-trailing gorilla arms to do it? And try, for once, to actually do a decent job.'

It was hardly Dorothy Parker and the Algonquin Round Table but it passed the time.

A week later we decided to whitewash the low ceiling of the shed. Philip — must I mention this? — was forced to stand on a milk crate in order to reach the roof.

Philip: 'Why are you painting faster than me?'

Me: 'Because I'm a person of decent height. I don't have to keep moving the box every time I do a new bit.'

Philip: 'Get fucked. Fuck off.'

Me: 'You're up and down on that thing like a newlywed's nightie.'

Philip: 'At least my knuckles don't trail along the ground. How many days has it been since you learnt to walk erect?'

Me: 'Fuck off. Get fucked.'

Philip: 'Stop painting so quickly, you prehensile monkey. Your work is really shoddy. You're dripping everywhere.'

(Pause.)

Me: 'Do you want me to paint your bald scone while I'm up here? Might help keep the sun off it.'

Philip: 'Fuck off and stop fucking dripping.'

(Pause.)

Me: 'Why don't you clean up the drips for me? At your height, you're already pretty close to the ground ...'

Again, hardly sophisticated repartee, and maybe that's why no one has ever bothered to transcribe this stuff — the abusive backchat of the Australian building site. It's really just a form of background music designed to keep the vocal cords warm and to assist in workplace safety.

Workplace safety?

Oh yes. I was beginning to see the wisdom in some of the behaviour of the Australian male. The constant torrent of abuse is a sort of sonar signal, similar to that used by bats. The rich invective means you are constantly aware of where the other person is standing. No way are you going to swivel around with a spinning drill or plank of wood, not knowing he is there. Just think how many dangerous accidents have been avoided because the

'Me and Shorty' — the sophisticated repartee of the building site.

endless abuse alerted Builder Number One to the location of his pathetically short-arsed mate.

More important still, I found myself enjoying this new, robust, jokey world — quite different to the world of my adolescence, the sensitive, linguistically cautious world of Canberra Youth Theatre. I liked the aggressive swagger of it; the bluster; the bubbling camaraderie and good humour. I also liked the feeling of my body, getting stronger as we dug and lifted and sawed, as calluses developed on my hands and a surprising lump of muscle appeared on each of my arms. Philip was still the better builder. But I was picking up some skills.

←

Building a house seems an impossible task, but of course
you don't do it all at once — especially if you are a
weekend builder. When I told people I was building a
place in the country, nearly everyone asked the same
question: 'How do you know what to do?' The answer was
humdrum: we learnt one task at a time, with Philip
picking up the skill first, and then teaching it to me.

So far, we had learnt the right way to make mudbricks,
then the wrong way to dig footings. Next we had learnt
how to cut logs and bark them. At each stage, we'd read a
chapter or two of a book before having a chat to someone
who looked like they knew something. Then we'd proceed
by trial and error. Error, mostly, but usually not for long.
For me, it was a revelation: suddenly I realised I could
handle tools and achieve a result. I'm not claiming I did
the work well, but if your standards are low enough ...

This, I was beginning to understand, was one of the
great things about a bush house. Up here you could have
a go at things in a way you'd never dare try at home in the
city. If the job went badly and the result was not pretty,
there was a litany of excuses on hand. Philip would
wander over to where I'd completely botched a job and
smile happily.

'I've buggered it,' I'd admit.

'Well,' he'd reply, 'it's not meant to be fine cabinet
work.'

My errors of craftmanship — and more rarely his — were so common that we developed quite a selection of excuses. (Please feel free to make use of them during your own building projects.)

- 'No one's going to be staring at that bit of the wall.'
- 'It'll make it look rustic.'
- 'Well, we're not looking for some sort of sterile brick veneer.'
- 'That bit will be behind a pole.'
- Or — our personal favourite — 'It's not meant to be the ceiling of the Sistine Chapel.'

They say that Persian weavers always include one mistake when they make a carpet; it's so they don't offend God by pretending that humans can achieve perfection. If that's right then God must have been particularly contented by the sight of our early workmanship on the mud house.

Yet for all its mistakes, the work made me feel good about myself. The cloud of self-doubt that had hovered over me since teenage years was starting to dissipate. I loved using a plane and watching the peel of wood curling elegantly upwards. The joy of striking a nail oh-so-sweetly into the grain with one perfectly timed blow. The flush of pleasure when you construct — or, in my case, chance upon — a mitred joint that fits as snugly as two lovers. Maybe I'd finally found an OK way to be a bloke — a positive male identity that came when you pulled on your paint-spattered work shorts; a vision of manliness that was positive and creative, unconnected with the negatives that had become, however stupidly, associated in my mind with masculinity.

←

By midway through the second year, we had close to half the mudbricks we needed — about 1500 of them. We'd cut and barked the tree poles needed. And we'd given up on the idea of digging the foundations by hand. While the laborious excavation of the bathroom had been a success, the trenches for the foundations had collapsed one time too many. We now planned to save up the cash and order both a backhoe and concrete truck, and knock off the foundations in one go.

We did seem to have a little more money. I was 28 years old, had finished a cadetship in journalism, and was writing longer pieces for Sydney's main broadsheet newspaper, mostly about theatre and film. Debra was writing plays but also some TV shows, such as *Sweet and Sour*, *Palace of Dreams* and even *Bananas in Pyjamas*. Occasionally cheques would arrive for her, which I would feverishly convert into their equivalent in terms of concrete.

Philip, always fascinated by politics, had landed himself a job working for Senator John Button, the popular trade minister in the Hawke and Keating governments. To the rest of us, it seemed an unspeakably glamorous job. At one point Phil accompanied Button to the funeral of the Soviet leader Konstantin Chernenko. With his usual confidence he joined the line of world leaders, somewhere between Margaret Thatcher and George Bush Senior, and shook the hand of Chernenko's successor. It was a very Philip thing to do. If only they'd known how stupid he was about the role of roof angle in the collection of rainwater in the Australian bush.

Around this time, Debra and I moved out of our share house and into the first place of our own — a small flat in Kings Cross on the edge of Sydney's red-light district. Peter Stiff, our rodeoing neighbour, thought this was a pretty hilarious address. Almost immediately our bush block was given the name Kings Cross, as in the phrase 'What are they doing up there at Kings Cross?' or 'I stopped in and had dinner up there at Kings Cross'. There was many a mention of the brothel we no doubt intended to establish on the site. Peter reckoned one delighted old local had asked him, 'How much do you'd reckon they'd charge a fella?'

Not only did Debra and I have a new flat, I was convinced that, educated by Philip, I now had the skills to renovate it. I decided to start with the kitchen, installing cork tiling, new benchtops and an ironing centre of my own design — a contraption of some beauty, which would swivel down from the wall revealing a power point and neatly chiselled starch holder.

'When not in use it will just fold away,' I said to Debra, gesturing grandly at the blank piece of wall where it would soon sit.

Within a few weeks I had completed one of the world's great acts of DIY — Destroy It Yourself. Almost everything I'd touched was now worse than when I'd begun. I had a particular problem with the new benchtop. Due to some inaccurate sawing, there were gaps in the thing big enough to lose a spoon in.

The ironing centre board, it turned out, wobbled so furiously during use that it was impossible to use for actual ironing, although it was possible to use it very gently to fold the odd T-shirt.

I was forced to have recourse to the Fuckwit Range of Fillers — those tubes of cover-all goo sold in suburban hardware stores. All have these optimistic product names such as No More Holes! and Fills All Gaps! and You'll Never Notice It's Not Wood!, and have prospered on the basis of making wild promises to idiots. No proper handyman would ever buy this junk. A proper handyman might purchase a single tube of wood-filler to putty up the nail holes in his beautifully constructed wooden blanket box; but I was buying this stuff by the barrow load. By the time I'd finished, the kitchen mainly consisted of cheap wood-filler. It was the chief building material. This left the room with two problems: one was the lingering odour; the other was the way the whole place shrank in cold weather.

It was times like this that the apprentice carpenter had an urge to blame his tools. I know everyone says, 'It's a bad workman that blames his tools', but in my case the tools really were terrible. Aussie men of past generations were famous for their ability to fix anything. 'All Auntie Vera had to do was point out the problem and Uncle Frank could fix it,' Auntie Vera's relatives would boast. But look at Uncle Frank's tools. The man had a shed. With power. The shed had a fridge. He had copies of *Australasian Post* in there. And his own body weight in high-class chisels. No wonder he could fix stuff.

I, by contrast, had the hall cupboard, down the back of which, once I'd moved the vacuum cleaner to one side and rifled through the spare sleeping bags, I would find a sad and tangled pile of cheap tools, many of them purchased from the bargain bin outside Clint's Crazy Bargains. There were chisels which, for want of anything better, I'd attempted to use as screwdrivers. Set squares that I'd used as paint-tin openers. And a socket set I'd once pressed into service as a hammer.

Working with this gear, even Uncle Frank would have needed an endless tube of Hides All Errors.

←

Despite the state of our kitchen, life in the city was fun. As friends moved up to Sydney from Canberra, we'd find them flats in the buildings on either side of our block. Within a year, it felt like we knew half the street.

Debra wrote a play called *Dags*, which turned out to be quite a hit; there was a national tour and even the odd largish cheque. (Again: royalties at 10 percent multiplied by an audience of 350 = 2.5 cubic metres of concrete.) At work, I'd taken on the role of the reporter who did humiliating things in order to get a laugh. I appeared on a TV show called *Perfect Match*, and another called *Star Search*. I interviewed Miss Piggy and other visiting fictional characters. I even wrote a feature on Sydney's lovers' lanes, which involved marching up to cars with steamy windows and asking the occupants their opinion of this particular lovers' lane. It was very surprising that I wasn't killed.

I also got the chance to fill in as a night-time presenter on ABC radio, and loved the experience, even amid the terror of it all. My first show involved an interview about the Romanian dictator Nicolae Ceausescu. I practised my pronunciation as the clock ticked down: 'Cheesequecow ... Cowquestkoo ... Choosesquuse.' There was no way I could get it right. The show started, I played a song and then conducted a 15-minute interview in which I asked questions about the death of the late Romanian dictator, about the wife of the former Romanian dictator, and about the arrest of the son of the deposed leader, all without once mentioning his name. Verbally incompetent? Yes, but also canny.

The second interview was a report about Australia's preparations for the Olympics; a terrifying prospect for someone who knew nothing about sport. The producer typed a note on the computer screen indicating I should ask about the champion walker Kerry Saxby. I deepened my voice to suggest the locker-room machismo which I imagined was appropriate to a sports report, combined with a tone that indicated Saxby and I were best mates: 'So, Kerry Saxby — how's he going?'

'Well,' said the sport reporter, without missing a beat, '*she's* going really well.'

Through the control-room screen I could see the producer's face, and could read the thought bubble that had just emerged over her head: 'Sure he's got a good face for radio, but what are we going to do about the brain?'

←

After some diligent saving — and by raiding Debra's royalties from *Dags* — we eventually had the cash to install the foundations. Here was another revelation about building: when you look at a house you only see what's above the ground. I was discovering that 20 percent of the work is buried beneath the surface.

The backhoe arrived. After months in which I'd toiled with shovel and pick for almost no result, the backhoe operator did the job in a little over three hours, producing a series of crisp trenches into which we installed a mesh of steel reinforcing. The cement trucks arrived and pumped out a cascade of concrete. An hour later they were gone — leaving perfect foundations. Now, why hadn't we thought of doing it that way first time around?

We left the foundations to dry and got on with other work. We ordered a truckload of fired bricks with which to build the footings and the chimney. We also set about making the remaining 2000 mudbricks.

A month later, a truck lumbered up from the Bowral brickworks and hoisted two pallets of fired bricks onto the edge of the building site. We signed a cheque which, given our experiences at the mud pits, seemed an easy way to secure 1000 bricks.

Two years after we had bought the place, we were now ready to start real building — laying the five courses of fired brick which would lift the mudbricks clear of the ground.

Again we hit the books and emerged with a new vocabulary of brick-laying terms — of header bricks and

Philip and I — the bricklayers at their craft.

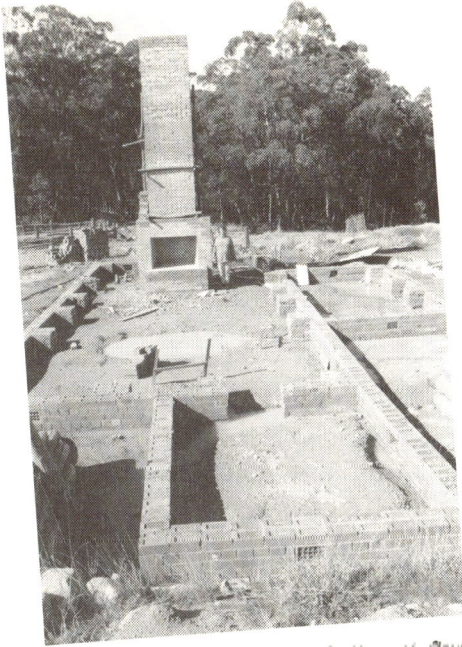

The outline of the house, built with five courses of fired brick.

stretcher bricks, of queen closers and sailors. We learnt to use a brick chisel, cracking the bricks in half in order to create a bonded wall — one in which the bricks are staggered so that mortar joints don't line up. We also became dab hands at 'pointing' the wall — cleaning away the mortar where it has extruded between the bricks, then running a tool along the joint to create a neat finish.

The footings were relatively easy. The chimney was tougher — six metres high and around 70 courses (or rows) of brick. For the first couple of metres we could work off ladders but what then? Our finances were improving, but we still couldn't afford to buy or hire scaffolding.

Work paused for a couple of weeks while Philip went overseas with Senator Button. The trip included Hong Kong, and Philip returned with a Big Idea. In the Hong Kong building industry they used bamboo scaffolding. Even skyscrapers were built using it — lengths of bamboo tied together with wire, creating what he called 'a very safe scaffold'. Why couldn't we do the same thing using the branches of gum trees?

In retrospect, a number of answers suggest themselves:

- Because bamboo is flexible while eucalyptus is brittle.
- Because bamboo is straight while eucalyptus mostly isn't.
- Because the people building the scaffold have been doing it for centuries and know what they are doing, while you just came up with the idea because you had too many beers on the flight back.

Instead of which I said: 'Yeah, that'll work.'

We headed into the bush and cut up some saplings. With these we built a sort of climbing frame next to the chimney, the saplings tied together with fencing wire. As the chimney got higher so would the scaffold. It looked spectacularly dangerous, like a watchtower built by beavers.

We swung ourselves onto the frame using a ladder, then clambered onto the groaning structure. On top of

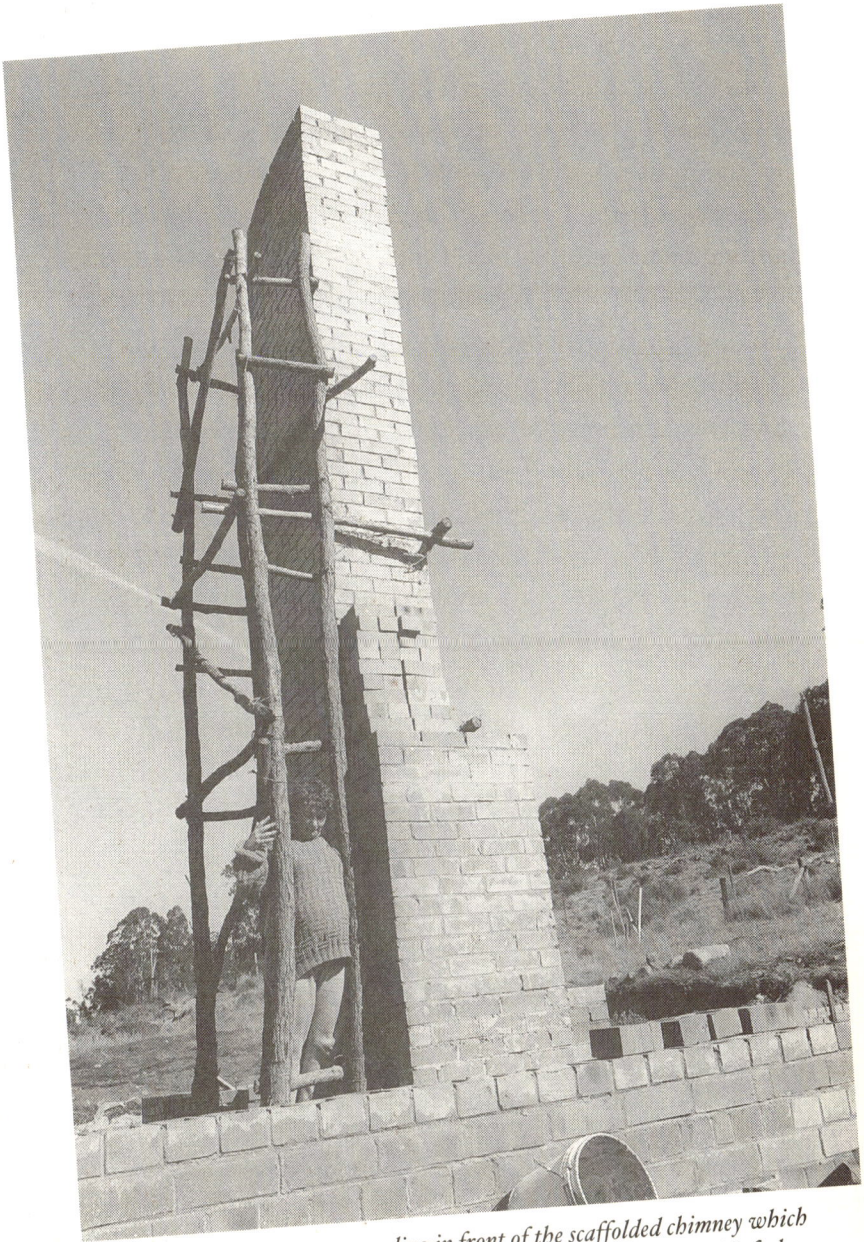

Debra, pregnant with Dan, standing in front of the scaffolded chimney which miraculously failed to kill the child's father.

the lot, we balanced a plank of wood to create a platform on which to stand. It felt shocking to be up there. Worse, you needed constant supplies of bricks and mortar. So the High Guy sent down a bucket tied to a piece of rope, which was filled with bricks and mortar by the Ground Guy, at which point the High Guy pulled the heavy bucket upwards — the scaffold shaking with every heave.

Debra, now pregnant with our first child, threw herself into the hard physical labour. Philip and I would take turns climbing the scaffold, while Debra worked on the ground — fetching water, mixing the mortar, carrying the bricks. I'd see her standing back, watching me on the scaffold as I heaved the bucket upwards, the scaffold creaking. There was a look of intense worry on her face. She knew this house was important. But a living father for her unborn child would also be a good thing.

After a few months of weekend effort, the chimney and footings were completed and we didn't have a single injury. Phil's eucalyptus scaffolding held firm. Not that I recommend anyone try it. A photograph shows Debra, seven or eight months into her pregnancy, standing under the scaffolding, the chimney stack behind her, six metres tall and pretty much straight and true. The scene is pregnant with possibility.

EIGHT

There was a storm of changes coming the way of the four builders. Philip's relationship with Gillian was at an end. They turned up together one day to tell us the news, both heartbroken. Gillian would sell Philip her interest in the project. Meanwhile, Debra and I had moved house, from Kings Cross to the slightly more sedate inner-city suburb of Marrickville. We had a baby on the way.

At work I'd been given the job of news editor — one of those nightmare positions in which you can easily work from eight in the morning until 11 at night. Debra was unimpressed by the hours, and unimpressed by the pumped-up, anxious personality the work left in its wake.

Debra's pregnant belly continued its steady expansion. She was on deadline with a play and a television script, but had reserved the fortnight before the birth to clean out the old disused kitchen of the house. She was going to set it up as her office.

'You can do the heavy lifting and scrub out the grease,' she instructed, 'but I'll do the rest.'

It was an act of self-confidence; a way of affirming she'd be able to combine her writing career and first-time motherhood. She purchased the raw materials — cork tiles for the floor, paint, a dark stain for the woodwork. Then suddenly the baby arrived — two weeks early, in a rush of burst waters during a rerun of *I Claudius*. We scrambled to the hospital and Daniel was born on 18 September 1987; the only time in his life he's been early for an appointment.

It was a caesarean delivery and Debra was stuck in hospital for over a week, nursing both her baby and herself. The next morning I woke up in the empty house and saw the room where the office was meant to be. It looked particularly sad.

Naturally, I decided to fix up the room. I also decided to make it a surprise. I figured it would give her a thrill when she came home.

I set the alarm each morning at dawn and threw myself into the renovations. Armed with bush-block confidence, I ripped out the old lino flooring, sugar-soaped the walls and applied litres of dark mahogany stain. I replaced a broken window and began installing the new cork-tile floor. This time around I was not doing too bad a job.

After a few hours of renovating, I'd run into the newspaper office, spend the day amid the hysteria of the news desk, and then head to the hospital by 9pm. I'd walk in, sit on the side of Debra's bed, then keel over. Ten minutes after arriving I'd be fast asleep, laid out along the edge of her narrow hospital bed.

At first she'd prod me awake. 'I can't believe you're the one acting tired. I'm the one who's just had a baby. All you've done is sit at a desk. Wake up.'

'Mrgh, yeah, arggh. Give me a second.'

I'd lift up my head then collapse again, shattered.

As I slept, Debra began to examine me. She noticed the strange brown splodges on my arms.

'He's so sleepy,' she would think, 'and with these brown lesions all over his arms. It's some terrible disease. He's dying. Leaving me with a baby to raise on my own.'

She'd sob quietly.

Worse, each day, I'd be sleepier, with even more brown splotches. They were now appearing on my neck and face. Open sores had also appeared on my hands, a product of my attempts to fix the window, but she wasn't to know that. Clearly the child would be fatherless within days.

A week later she came home. The office was finished, with a big red bow stuck on the door and a banner saying, 'Welcome home Debra'. I smiled slyly and watched as she pushed open the door.

She walked in, circled around, took it all in, delighted. I'd sanded and resurfaced her desk and it gleamed in the sun. The cork-tile flooring was less perfect but not a bad effort.

She looked up at me and burst into happy tears. It was a heartfelt response, I imagined, to my superb carpentry. Helped just a little, perhaps, by the revelation I wasn't dying.

←

Dan's birth — like that of many first children — brought fresh priorities. I vowed (successfully) to give up smoking. I vowed (unsuccessfully) to limit my drinking. I also knew I'd have to find a less insane job at the newspaper. After about nine months I managed to grab one. I'd be European correspondent, living in London. Most of the time the hours would be vaguely normal. I could give Debra and Daniel their due. The only downside: the bush house. The project would have to be put on hold while we were away. Philip could make a few bricks solo, but it would be impossible for him to tackle the next big job: the building of the wooden frame. The house would have to wait.

The work in England was enjoyable. It stretched my skills — I was forced to write about politics, business, even sport. Debra, separated from her connections with Australian theatre and television, wrote a novel for children. We made some British friends. There was something about Debra's mixture of vulgarity and intellectualism they found — to use their word — 'refreshing'. I formed the view that the men all had the hots for her.

The two of us spent a lot of time talking about the bush block — picturing that brick chimney poking upwards, awaiting the house that would form around it. I remember standing in the kitchen of the London house, a grey sky out the window, weeping over a cassette-tape recording of John Williamson's 'Cootamundra Wattle', and thinking about the wattle trees we'd planted on the block. Oh yes, I had it bad. As soon as it was decent — when 14 months had passed — we elected to return home.

←

A few days after we arrived back in Australia, we headed up for a weekend at the block: Debra, me and Dan, who was about to turn two. We drove up on a wintry Friday night, and parked the car so I could put up the tent using the headlights. We'd decided the baked-bean caravan was too small for even two adults and a baby. As I started putting up the tent, it began to snow. Our tent was easy to erect — especially by a team of ten, on a windless day, in full sunshine. It was less easy at night with a gathering snowstorm and a toddler turning blue.

'Just hurry up,' Debra wailed, stamping her feet warm. 'Your son is turning blue.'

'Can you just give me a moment?' I pleaded. I was holding the roof up with one hand and had a guy rope gripped between my teeth, so what I actually said was, 'Cang oo ust ive me ah oment.'

I fixed the front of the tent into an upright position then moved to the rear. By the time I got there, the front had collapsed. This process continued until about 1am, at which point the car lights failed, due to a technical problem known to mechanics as 'a flat battery'.

Debra: 'I think the battery is flat.'

Richard: 'Well, that would explain why we are standing in the dark.'

Any possibility of motorised escape having been denied, I somehow forced the tent into an upright position. We crawled in and I tried to sleep, disturbed by nothing save the melodious howling of the wind, the fortissimo chattering of Debra's teeth and the sobbing of the baby. This character-building situation continued until 3.30am, at which point the tent collapsed.

Maybe England hadn't been so bad.

I awoke to the feeling of damp, snow-heavy canvas against my cheek and a cold metal pole spearing into my ribs. I groped for the tent's doorway. This was when I discovered that the tent had blown over onto its side; the ceiling was now the floor, and the door which I was having trouble opening was, in fact, the sewn-shut window.

Debra held the damp canvas off Dan's face while I concentrated on panicking.

The chance of locating a torch in this damp morass of upturned bags, wailing toddler, leaking water bottles and broken Primus lamps was slight. So was the possibility of locating my shoes, which is how I came to be standing in bare feet, ankle-deep in snow, at 3.45am, attempting to re-erect a tent in the face of the howling wind that knocked it down in the first place. It was at this point I began whimpering.

Let me check the word in the dictionary so I'm sure it's the right one: 'crying with low, plaintive sounds, as a child'. Yes, that's the one.

In the end I got the tent back up; baby Dan was unscathed; and we all slumped back into sleep. The snowstorm, however, did press the issue: it would be good to have an actual building up here.

←

Over the next month Philip and I consulted the plans and ordered the hardwood for the frame. It came to about $4000. We both decided to take a week off work, pledging ourselves to an impossible timetable. Counting the weekends on either side, we had nine days to construct the basic wooden outline of the house — installing the tree poles we'd cut four years before, the ridge beam and the perimeter beam, which we'd build out of new timber, but not the rafters, which could be left until later.

At this point more seasoned builders might scoff and question my apprehension. Two blokes, a relatively small building and nine days. It sounds like plenty of time. For them I have a response.

And that response is: no power tools.

Through a mixture of poverty and stupidity, we'd convinced ourselves that it was not worth the money to buy or hire a generator. Besides, who needs power tools? People for generations have been building using hand tools. Why not us? We'd have silence instead of a noisy generator, and the pleasure of working with timber in the traditional way — the sweet smell of sawdust created by one's own sweat.

By 7am on Saturday morning we were lifting our first length of wood onto the sawhorse. Philip marked it up and I moved in with my handsaw, pulling it against the wood, trying to start the cut.

The saw was skittish, shuddering off the line.

'Just do it gently, you gorilla,' Philip chided. 'You are pushing down too hard.'

'Fuck off.'

He had shown me how to do this when we built the shed. I knew the method. Push down too hard and the teeth of the saw get jammed in the wood. You've got to let the saw do the work.

Philip stood behind, assessing my attempts. 'You've got to let the saw do the work.'

'I know that. You told me before. Fuck off.'

The saw settled down and began to create a neat groove in the wood.

'The saw has found its groove,' I marvelled. 'It's so groovy it's cutting edge!'

'Just saw the wood, you gorilla.'

Finally the offcut fell to the ground. It had taken

about two minutes to make just one cut in one plank. I was also slightly out of breath.

Philip slapped me merrily on the back. 'People pay good money for exercise like this.'

←

In retrospect, using hand tools was an act of self-defeating insanity. Drilling a single hole in hardwood took several minutes of grinding away with a brace and bit. Just sawing a piece of wood to length was a whole cardio workout. Later I read a book called *The Owner-Built Home* and found a statistic: cutting all the two-by-fours for the frame of a small house takes seven days using a handsaw and only 30 minutes with a power saw.

After three days we'd installed only about a third of the tree poles — connecting them up with sections of perimeter beam as we went. Five days in and we were still less than halfway there. Every task took twice the time we'd allocated. We also had to assemble the ridge beam — starting with the crossbeams which would connect it to the tree poles. There was a lot of precise carpentry involved. Our real problem was that we'd booked a crane to arrive on the seventh day: its job was to lift the ridge beam into place. If the frame wasn't finished, we'd do our dough: $1000 for the crane hire.

We began getting up at 6am and working until it was dark. My forearms looked like I had a heroin addiction —

*Building the frame ... why
are these guys so worried?*

covered in bruises plus pinpricks of blood from heaving rough hardwood. Every night I would go to bed with my body aching.

The crane was due at 9am on Saturday morning. We finished the necessary work an hour before it arrived. Philip, normally so confident, was nervous. 'It's not going to fit.'

He stared at the ridge beam, his lips clamped down in a tense grimace. 'Six points. It's got to slot in perfectly at six separate points. If just one of them is out, we're stuffed.'

I was forced to do duty as the optimist. 'We measured five times over. We measured the poles. We measured the ridge assembly. We checked it. It will work.'

'But what if it doesn't? Once the crane is here, you can't take down the poles and start again. It's $1000, just gone. How frustrating will that be?'

'You're talking as if the bad thing has already happened. Can we at least wait for the bad news to actually occur before we both enter the kingdom of despair?'

Phil agreed this seemed a reasonable plan.

Debra arrived just before the crane, bringing Philip's new partner, Diana, Michael, the owner of the baked-bean caravan, and my old school friend Simon — a doctor, which could be useful. There was also young Dan — a toddler in an engineer's hard-hat. I have photos of us all from that morning including one of Philip and I staring nervously at the frame.

The crane began to do its work. Michael and Simon hung off the frame like monkeys, ready to bolt off at all six meeting points. The guy who came with the crane was higher still, while Philip and I supervised from the ground. Having endured the Hong Kong scaffolding, we seemed to have developed an affection for terra firma.

The crane lowered the ridge assembly towards the frame. 'It's not going to fit,' said Phil.

The driver lowered it a little closer. 'It's not going to fit,' said Phil.

It now came within a half-metre. The crane operator was going slowly, trying to line up the six slots with the six tree poles. 'I think it's going to fit,' said Phil.

Lower, lower, lower. And in, at all six points. It was a perfect fit. Philip hooted with relief. We all let loose a cheer. Maybe we were not so incompetent after all.

Phil and I pledged to return the next weekend and begin the task of installing the 34 roof rafters, the heavy beams of hardwood that connected the ridge beam to the perimeter beam. It was a new task and, as usual, we had no idea how it might be achieved. Without a crane, it was hard to imagine how they could possibly be lifted into place.

←

It was dusk. A week on. And something truly dangerous was about to occur. Phil and I were on our own. If Debra was here this would not have been happening. If anyone

The ridge beam is dropped into place ... will it connect up at all six points?

Yes! It fits! Next the bolting off.

sensible were here this would not have been happening. I was sitting in the driver's seat of my car, parked in the field next to the house. The window was wound down so I could hear instructions from outside. The car engine was ticking over.

Philip was sitting on top of the ridge beam, six metres up, his legs dangling down, his hands gripping the wood. He looked pretty nervous.

'OK,' he yelled, 'a tiny bit of acceleration. Just creep forward very slowly.'

I let off the handbrake and pressed down very gently on the accelerator. A rope was tied onto my towbar, and as I edged forward it became taut.

The rafters — each one had to be pulled up using ropes ...

'Stop now,' yelled Philip, panic in his voice.

The rope rose into the air from my towbar, went up over the ridge beam, just near where Phil was sitting, then headed downwards and over the far perimeter beam. From there it hung to the ground where it was tied to a heavy rafter. We hoped to use the car and the rope to pull the rafter up and into place. There was a possible hitch: the sideways pressure on the frame would pull over the whole house, destroying all our work so far and bringing about Philip's violent, and yet spectacular, death.

'OK, very gently,' Philip instructed.

I pressed down again on the accelerator. The tautness of the rope increased and the wooden frame creaked sharply. It was a sort of yelping noise.

'Stop,' shouted Philip, the word punching the air.

I put on the handbrake and jumped out of the car.

'It's just creaking,' I yelled. 'You'd expect it to creak.'

'Easy to say,' said Philip, 'if you're the one on the ground.'

'I'll just go forward another metre. Is that OK?'

'OK, but slow.'

I pressed on the accelerator and the car crept forward. The rope began to pull the rafter up, across the perimeter beam and into the air. It shuddered forward like a shaken finger pointed at the sky.

'Keep going,' yelled Phil.

I was driving with the car door open, my body turned to watch the action. I had one hand on the handbrake ready to stop, the other on the wheel. The rafter wobbled towards Phil.

'Now stop.'

I put the brake on and ran around to help. By means of a ladder, I could push upwards on the rafter, making the fit as tight as possible so that Phil could nail off.

'How am I meant to do this?' he asked, shouting down to me. I could see him squeezing his thighs against the ridge beam. He'd pulled a hammer from his tool belt and held it loosely in his right hand.

He also needed a second hand to hold onto the ridge beam so he didn't fall. And a third hand to lift the rafter upwards so it was flush. And a fourth hand to hold the nail in place ready for hammering. Then he'd be able to belt the nail into place using arm number one. It struck me: I didn't need a co-builder; I needed a four-armed Hindu deity.

Vishnu would do.

'You should be Vishnu. Vishnu could do it.'

'Vish-who? Just push upwards, you moron.'

'Vish-nu. He's a four-armed Hindu deity. I'm just trying to help.'

'As soon as I get down from here, I am going to kill you and scatter your corpse, so that birds can feed on it.'

Actually, I wasn't enjoying my own role in this. I was standing on a very rickety ladder with the free end of the rafter spearing into my shoulder as I tried to push it upwards. 'You know,' I shouted to Phil, 'it's quite tough being down here.'

At this point there was silence. It is possible that Phil had actually had enough of me.

I looked up and he was certainly focused on the task. He'd somehow lodged a nail into the right place and, taking his hand off the ridge beam, rapidly hammered it in. I could see he was squeezing his legs even tighter, trying to maintain his balance as he swung the hammer. He followed up with a few more nails until the thing was secured. I then nailed off the bottom end. A very shaky Philip swung himself off the ridge beam and onto the Hong Kong scaffolding.

'Good job,' I trilled when he finally reached the ground. 'Only 33 more to go.'

'One day I really will kill you,' is all he replied.

We repeated the process the next day and then the next weekend and then the weekend after that. It took several months of scattered visits to lift all the rafters into place. Sometimes, shamed by my fear, I'd insist on a turn at the high work. It was a sickening feeling — one hand holding the heavy rafter in place, the other holding onto the ridge beam.

'How does it feel now, Vishnu?' Phil would mock from below.

Eventually I realised you didn't have to be Vishnu; you just had to conquer your fear and trust to your mate below. So Phil would push upwards with the rafter, I'd take a hammer in one hand, a nail in the other, and squeeze my thighs around that ridge beam like a jockey on an enormously thin horse.

Whenever I mention I've built a mudbrick house, people always remark on the work that must be involved in making the bricks. But for this house, it was the wooden frame that nearly killed us — figuratively and literally. It took about six months to finish the roof — rafters, then battens, then the sheets of Zincalume.

←

At the end of this process we had something that looked like a house. The four of us — Debra and me, Philip and Diana — stood and admired our work. Sure, it was a house without walls and floor, but a house nonetheless.

'Let's move in,' suggested Philip.

'You might not have noticed,' observed Debra, 'but it doesn't have a floor. Just mud.'

Phil threw an arm around Debra's shoulder, like an overly friendly estate agent. 'Ah, yes, madam, but there's a fire. And a roof to keep off the rain. And because there's no floor, the fireplace opens at waist height — perfect for cooking.'

He had a point. We decided we would sleep in the tents but spend our evenings in the shell of our house, and the next weekend we arrived with furniture purchased from St Vincent de Paul — two mangy armchairs, a couch and an old table. We installed them all in front of the fireplace.

'Glass of wine, old boy?' proposed Phil from his armchair. He had the air of a British gentleman relaxing

*We moved in ... first without walls, and then the walls
were added. Who needs a floor?*

in front of the fire at his ancient and exclusive club. His boots and pants were splattered with mud.

'Shiraz or cabernet?' I inquired.

'A lively Barossa shiraz, I think, is in order,' he replied, straining to see me over his shoulder.

There'd been some squally weather recently, which had driven rain into the house, so the ground was a little wet. The back legs of his armchair, I noticed, had sunk deeply into the mud, giving the chair a jaunty, and possibly more comfortable, angle.

'I'll join you,' I said. I grabbed a bottle and two glasses, and slung myself into the other mud-marooned chair. It settled into the ground with a squelching noise as I added my weight.

The fire was stoked and blazing. Young Dan was asleep on a lilo, carefully lodged on a dry bit of ground. Debra and Diana were talking on the couch. Every time I glanced over at them, they appeared a little lower, their couch sinking slowly into the sodden ground. Wind and rain buffeted us from the side. But at least we'd have dinner in an hour or so, served indoors.

Here was joy. We were pigs in mud. Real mud.

NINE

During breaks in the building work, Debra and I would march over the block with Dan in a backpack, his eyes peering over my shoulders. It was great country for bushwalking — scrambling down to the tiny creeks and then clambering over a hill into the next valley. From the top of the hills the view would open up, and to the west you could see the green patch of the Wombeyan Caves Reserve, down in the valley. A neighbour, Jon Lewis, was fascinated by the Aboriginal history of the area and supplied me with details from obscure books he'd found in the library recording the creation story of the local Gundungurra people. As we rambled around the district with Dan, Jon's notes provided an alternative map.

There are various versions of the tale — but all seem to derive from an account recorded by the anthropologist RH Mathews in 1908, after meeting with a group of local

The view from near our block, down towards the Wollondilly River.

Aborigines camped by the Wollondilly River. The locals explained to Mathews how the landscape had been created during a great battle between two creatures — a huge animal, part fish and part reptile, known as Gurangatch; and an equally enormous tiger cat called Mirragan.

Mathews, in his essay for the *Zeitschrift für Ethnologie* recounts how these creatures had both human attributes and magical powers. 'They could make rivers and other geographical features, cleave rocks and perform many similar Herculean labours.' As Mirragan chased the Gurangatch, the landscape was formed — the frightened fish-reptile tearing up the ground to get away, in the process forming the bed of the Wollondilly, and then creating part of the Guineacor River. The story describes the drama, battle by battle, explaining the creation of the sharp loop in the Wollondilly, just south of the Wollondilly Nature Reserve, as well as the formation of Jocks Creek, the stream on which Granny Lang's first hut was built:

> Gurangatch then returned home along his burrow to the Wollondilly ... coming to a very rocky place which was hard to excavate, he changed his mind and ... made a long, deep bend or loop in the Wollondilly which almost doubles back upon itself at that place. When Gurangatch got down to where Jock's Creek now embouchures with the Wollondilly, he turned up Jock's Creek excavating a watercourse for himself. Being a great magician he could make the water flow uphill as easily as downhill.

The battle continued westward: the fish-reptile going underground, forming the Wombeyan Caves, while the cat was above, trying to spear Gurangatch through the rock using a massive pole. Here's where the story is at its most intoxicating: climb up on the ridge above the caves today and you see a sequence of holes that look exactly like those you'd expect from the story — as if a giant stake has been pushed into the earth many times.

> Gurangatch burrowed under the range, coming up in the inside of Wam'-bee-ang caves, which are called Whambeyan by the

white people, being a corruption of the
Aboriginal name ... Mirragañ did not care to
go into any of the subterranean passages,
therefore he went up on top of the rocks and
dug a hole as deep as he could go and then
prodded a long pole down as far as it would
reach, for the purpose of frightening
Gurangatch out of his retreat, much in the
way we poke a kangaroo rat or other creature
out of a hollow log.

There's plenty more in the story: the tiger cat ends up
going home, where he gets into trouble with his wife for
chasing the poor fish. He takes no notice of her, sets off
again and finally catches up with Gurangatch at a place
called Slippery Rock — their long battle there being the
thing that made the surface so smooth. They then head
into the Blue Mountains, forming the landscape around
Katoomba, before Gurangatch heads underground once
again — this time creating the Jenolan Caves. After a few
more scuffles, the exhausted combatants call it a day,
both sides returning to their families and leaving a
landscape created by their travails.

While we bushwalked through the hills, noting the
scenes of Mirragan and Gurangatch's war, the landscape
created in more recent times was experiencing its own

battles. The drought was worsening; small towns in particular were suffering economically. Taralga, our closest town, was going from bad to worse. When we'd first bought our block, there were still two pubs, a butcher and two general stores. Now, just six years on, the butcher was gone, one of the pubs was on death's door, and there was only one store. Occasionally a new business would open, stagger on for a month or two and then close. An example was Legends, a cafe which opened briefly in one of the bluestone houses in the main street. It had only one table and the cooking equipment comprised a single electric frypan, but one Saturday night, Philip and I walked in, both scrubbed up for a big night in town.

Philip placed the order. 'Two hamburgers with the lot.'

'Drinks?' asked the lady, hoping for a slightly larger order.

'We'll have a beer later at the pub.'

'Oh, alright.'

The walls were decorated with line drawings of what appeared to be famous movie stars. As we waited, Philip and I examined one of the images. We didn't say anything but we must have looked confused. The lady peered up from her frypan and offered an explanation. 'It's meant to be Frank Sinatra,' she said in a flattened monotone. 'I know it doesn't look anything like him.'

She sighed with disappointment. 'I got an artist in from Goulburn and everything.'

The hamburgers were terrific but, as we ate, the proprietor was still staring balefully at her walls, pointing to other 'legends' who gave her establishment its name.

'That one's Elvis, although you wouldn't know it,' she observed wearily.

'Oh, no, it's very like him,' Philip lied.

'And that one is meant to be James Dean,' she added, grimly wiping her hands on a cloth, 'although I don't suppose his own mother would recognise him.'

We finished our burgers and headed for the door, the woman still muttering about Goulburn and the standard of its illustrators. We headed up the road to the Argyle Inn. There an older woman was sitting at one of the tables in front of the fire, nursing a beer. I chatted to her as I waited for Phil to buy our drinks. She talked engagingly about her life and her recent move to Taralga.

'And why did you come to Taralga?' I asked politely.

'Oh, to die,' she chirped. 'The local cemetery is quite marvellous.'

She took a sip of her beer and then described the scenic qualities of the local Stonequarry Cemetery.

'It's up on Golspie Road,' she advised. 'You should take a look. Perfect place for when you're dead.'

I promised her I would check it out.

While Taralga was on its knees, with at least one of the locals waiting for death, Goulburn should have been a little more resilient. Goulburn was a big town — with a population of 20,000 and a claim to be Australia's first inland city. It was on the highway from Sydney to

Melbourne, and home to the Big Merino — a 15-metre-high fibreglass sheep, which tourists could enter via a door in the animal's bum. But the drought was hurting there as well. By 1991 they had the trifecta — drought, high interest rates and a collapse in wool prices.

Goulburn had a slightly desperate feel, as if the local business people were scratching their heads as to how to turn a buck. Phil and I would head down to search for building materials — in particular, the second-hand windows we'd need as soon as we started laying the mudbricks.

Our favourite business was in the industrial estate. It offered perhaps the oddest advertising sign I've ever seen, a big professionally drawn billboard, bolted to the cyclone mesh fence and reading in large bold capitals:

GRAVEL & SAND
BUILDING MATERIALS
AGRICULTURAL CHEMICALS
CHILDREN'S CLOTHES

Driving in through the gate, it was all there, spread out on the concrete apron — the stacks of blackened lumber, the bays of aggregate and sand, and — right in the middle — a single rack of pink jumpsuits and natty jackets. Why did the lumber yard stock a range of children's clothes? Who was the fast-talking salesman who had convinced the owner of the synergy that exists between children's clothes and used building materials? Who can say. At some point, for some reason, this place had taken delivery of a whole rack of kidswear and had been trying to move it ever since.

'What can I do you for today?' the attendant would ask gruffly, once you'd driven in. He never spelt out the full menu but the options were clear: a tonne of gravel, a stack of timber sleepers, and if we still had room on the back of the ute, what about a set of triple-o pastel playsuits? Over the years we went there, I saw this place sell any number of hardware items, but never anything from that rack of clothing.

One day the attendant who rolled up had a slightly plaintive edge to his negotiations, as if his next beer was dependent on whatever sale he could make in the following half hour. We asked if he had a chisel among his second-hand tools. 'No,' he said with some melancholy, as if he could see the beer disappearing into the distance. Then he brightened, struck by an idea. 'I could sell you my own.'

He went to his car, removed his toolbox, and wandered back with a decent-enough chisel. 'I'll give it to you for $5.'

I handed over the money. We drove off in Phil's ute but I found it hard to shake off the sadness of the transaction. 'It was his own chisel,' I pondered.

'He sold it,' replied Phil.

'Yeah, but just because he was desperate for a beer. He was looking at the $5 when I handed it to him as if it were already a glass of Toohey's.'

'He sold it,' insisted Phil.

'Yeah, but he was almost licking his lips. He could taste that beer.'

Phil turned in the driver's seat and gave me a 'grow-up' look. 'Just be thankful,' he said, 'you didn't ask him for a spare pair of undies, or he'd have stripped off on the spot and offered you his own.'

We rolled down the road with me laughing while Phil did impressions of the bloke stripping off all his clothes and selling them to us piece by piece. 'I'll give you these undies for $2, and would you boys be looking for a pair of socks, not too stinky ...?'

We headed down to the other demolition yard — a place called Trader Bob's, a bit closer to town, with a series of sheds full of stuff, including what seemed like the whole contents of a demolished hospital. If you needed 500 bedpans, an old X-ray machine and 27 hospital beds, then Bob was your man. He also had windows, lots of them. We bought a full set for the house — nine windows in all — for the bargain price of $600.

←

Back in Sydney another bargain presented itself. My friend Julie had been hired to shoot an advertisement for SPC baked beans; the script called for a suburban house with big front windows. Our Marrickville house had windows that were just right. The ad included a shot from inside the house — the view out the window to be filled entirely with cans of baked beans. It was something to do with Jack and the Beanstalk. Julie arranged for us to be paid a $700 fee for the use of the house. We would also get to keep the beans.

I got home one night after work to find the film crew packing up. The cans of beans were stacked in a solid wall across the front of the house. I knew they were planning a wall of cans but this was ridiculous: it covered the whole width of the building, from the ground to the eaves. Debra wandered out to find me staring agog at the barricade of beans.

'They've left the empty boxes in the kitchen. All we have to do is put them back in the boxes and we get to keep them'.

'How many cans are there?'

'According to Julie, there are 144 boxes of them.'

'Each box containing ...?' I asked.

'Each containing,' Debra continued, '24 cans. Which ...'

I ran into my bedroom and grabbed my calculator. 'That's 3456 cans of beans. We own 3456 cans of baked beans.'

'Yeah', cautioned Debra. 'But no one says we have to eat them all at once.'

'Which is just as well,' I agreed. 'Do you understand what eating 3456 cans of baked beans would do to you? It would cause death by farting. It would raise global methane levels. Sea levels would rise. There'd be mass extinctions. Among our neighbours, if nowhere else.'

Debra ignored my hysteria. 'It's OK,' she said. 'I have a plan.'

Both of us had worked as volunteer counsellers at the Wayside Chapel, a drop-in service that helped organise accommodation and other services for homeless people in Kings Cross. We'd be able to palm off at least 3000 cans on all the hostels and refuges we'd had contact with.

'Fair enough,' I told her, 'but it'll be a windy night on the streets of Sydney.'

'And,' Debra added, 'you can take the other 456 cans up to the land. You and Phil can eat them while you build.'

←

With the windows — and the beans — in hand, we started bricking up. Again, Philip and I had taken a week off work to complete the task. I'd come around to the idea of fuelling the week entirely on baked beans. They were the perfect match for mudbrick: a free food source to match the free building material. Strangely, Philip didn't react well.

'How many boxes have you got of those things?' he asked as I unloaded the ute.

'A dozen boxes. About 300 cans.'

'I don't mind them one meal a day,' he said, shaking his head, 'but I'm not going to eat them breakfast, lunch and dinner.'

'Too bad, it's all I brought.'

'You're mental.'

Pox-ridden, filthy and propelled by beans ... the slog of bricking up.

'I don't think you understand,' I answered, speaking slowly so he'd have a better chance of grasping my logic. 'They are free. It's free food.'

'You are such a stingy bastard.'

'Besides,' I said, 'they were in an ad, so they are kind of glamorous.'

'There'll be nothing glamorous when you're on the ground farting yourself to death.'

'Consider the protein,' I replied, carrying in the last box. 'If you eat up, you might finally grow to a decent height.'

'You,' he said, 'are a farting, tightarse gorilla.'

There was another problem during our week of labour: I'd never caught chickenpox when I was growing up. It chose to hit on day two of the bricklaying. My body became covered in these disgusting pustulant sores. They itched like crazy, while the virus left me feeling dizzy and wan. Phil was immune to the disease but not to my mood, which darkened the sicker I got. It also started raining heavily, the building site quickly turning into a mud pit. Each day blurred into the next — trudging through viscous sludge carrying bricks; the clay adhering to our boots, until each step involved lifting a whole cake of earth. It felt like wearing cement boots.

I spent my time covered in a combination of mud and chickenpox blisters — soaked to the skin, dizzy with illness, climbing up and down ladders hauling bricks, and — courtesy of the beans — farting almost constantly. With the mud, the illness and the regular explosive reports from all sides, it felt like the trenches of the Somme.

'I hope you're happy now,' whined Phil, as he let loose an incredible volley of farts from atop his ladder. It was so loud I'm pretty sure I heard an echo bouncing back off one of the nearby hills.

'The air propulsion is getting me up this ladder,' I replied as I climbed towards him, a mudbrick in my arms, leaving behind a trail of tiny explosions much like an outboard motor.

Debra and Diana arrived with fresh food on the weekend and we were able to lay off the beans. The rain stopped, the sun shone and my chickenpox began to subside. With the women's help, the job was pretty much finished by the end of the seven days. We now had walls, windows and a roof.

I stacked the remaining boxes of baked beans in the shed — next to the bag of cement and the boxes of nails — just another raw material for building. Each time we came up, it was an ambition to get rid of as many cans as possible. Thus energised, we put chimney tops atop the chimney, painted the lintels and installed the front door. As usual Philip and I bickered as we built — my book learning and anxiety fighting against his experience and can-do confidence. The pattern was nearly always the same: I would go along with his idea and then the doubt would start gnawing away. I'd fetch the building books. I'd then find proof that Phil's method would result in the whole thing collapsing and us all being tragically killed.

'According to this table, you need a lintel twice that thickness if you're trying to span over a metre.'

'That's not right. You're reading the table wrong.'

'I'm not reading it wrong.'

'Give me the book.'

I'd show him the book — pointing out the width of the window and running my finger down to the spot that gave the necessary dimensions of the lintel.

Phil would look suspicious, pull the book away from me and run his own finger down to the spot.

'You see?' I'd say. 'I was right.'

Phil would never miss a beat. 'Well, sure,' he would declare, 'that was the industry standard up to a few years ago. I mean this book is 10 years old, but, yeah, if you want to do it this way ...'

He would then cheerfully do it my way. One night, in the middle of a heated late-night argument about the next day's work, Philip reached for the bottle of scotch which was sitting on the table between us and lifted it up playfully as if to smash it over my head. Alas, the cap was off the bottle, with the result that he instead managed to empty the contents over his own head.

'Ah, bugger me,' he said. And as he sat there, the scotch dripping off the end of his nose, I saw something unique: could it be the look of defeat in Philip's eyes?

He stood up, wiped his face and then turned to face me.

'Anyway, as I was saying, you are totally wrong about that ridge beam ...'

I discovered we needed both our personalities to build this house: without Phil's confidence and bluster the project would never have got going. My anxiety would have eaten away at every decision; we'd never have picked up tools. And without my gnawing anxiety? Just too many mistakes — forgotten dampcourses, missed lintels, rafters cut to the wrong length.

We enjoyed some glorious days of building as we finished off the house, Philip making me laugh out loud — up a ladder, his shirt off, singing a made-up song: 'I'm Buck Naked the Builder, Buck Naked the Builder am I'. Or, after making a mistake, another joyous ditty sung at the top of his voice: 'Oh, Phil the Fuck-Up, that's my name, Fuck-Up Phil, that's my game'.

In the months that followed, we spent weekends installing the bearers for the floor and topping them with a cheap sheet flooring called yellow tongue. I was so thrilled by the new floor that, late on the night of its completion, I stripped off in tired, drunken glee and danced naked in front of the fire for the assembled crew. My ballet training lived on. How this performance was greeted is hard to remember; sharper is the memory of the splinter injury experienced by my bottom halfway through.

Finally we could lift our chairs out of the mud. We cleaned the dirt off the furniture and reinstalled it atop the neat chipboard floor. The interior ceiling was unfinished; there was no bathroom. We'd yet to build the loft bedrooms and the staircase that would lead up the

A house of sorts ... the bricking up is nearly finished.

them, but the house looked grand — like a small high-ceiled chapel of mud and wood.

From now on most of the work would be indoors, labouring in enclosed spaces. 'Maybe,' cautioned Phil, 'it's time to give the beans a rest.'

Bricking-up was finishing by the end of January 1993. We then built a bathroom off the side, occupying that gloriously flat piece of land we'd dug by hand all those years before. We could have used mudbricks — but mere mention of the brick pits created an aching sensation in all our backs. Instead we built stud walls, with planks of western red cedar on the outside and pine lining boards

Dan joins the building crew.

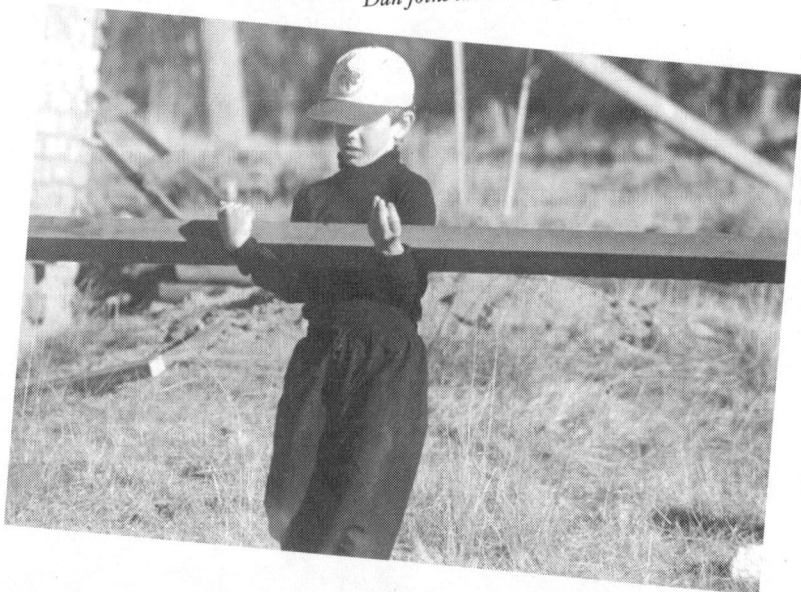

on the inside. We installed a toilet and a shower, both linked up to a septic tank. To clad the walls of the shower recess we used something called 'Mini Orb' — a miniature version of the material you use to create a tin roof.

We did a bad job on the tiling, but then again it was never meant to be the floor of the Sistine Chapel. Amazingly, it all worked — the gas-bottle hot water, the flush toilet, the taps and basin. No longer would morning ablutions require a long walk into the forest with a mattock slung over your shoulder. Even better, we could finally shower indoors — a dozen years after we bought the place. Denis the camp shower toddled off to enjoy a well-deserved retirement.

We then worked on the inside of the house, constructing a mezzanine hung off the perimeter beam, with two bedrooms nestled up into the ceiling, accessible by a simple staircase. We discovered that with sufficient sanding, the roughest Australian hardwood could produce a perfectly silky-smooth handrail.

We were now 11 years on from when we'd made our first brick. We'd spent the first five years making the bricks and building the foundations; taken a year off while Debra and I were in London; and then spent another five years building the frame, installing the roof, and laying the bricks. Dan was now eight years old, and we had a second child — Joe — still a baby. Phil and Di had married and also had two children, Olivia and Georgia. We now had a squad of navvies and we intended to use them — at least, those old enough to hold a hammer.

Over the next few years, we built a wooden deck on the front and back of the building, and panelled the walls of the bedrooms. Whenever possible, we set the kids to work: a row of them, nailing down decking, sawing lining boards for the bedrooms, or chopping wood for the fire.

Best of all, I watched Daniel fall in love with the place — buzzing as he worked alongside Phil, or exploring the bush with an old Akubra stuck on his head. He loved the Aboriginal creation story about Gurangatch and Mirragan, and convinced himself that the Slippery Rock featured in the story must be on our very block. There was, after all, a shelf of smooth rock down on one of our two creeks. He had just turned eight when he came back from a weekend in the bush and scratched out a simple poem about his experiences:

> I'd heard the Aboriginal story about
> Slippery Rock.
> Hoping, wanting, my heart was set on seeing it in
>   Real life.
>
> From our bush house
> We walked down the gully,
> Dad and me.
> The bush was rough and steep,
> Body tilted so my feet didn't slip.
>
> Down and
> Down
> Then there's flatness.

Beautiful spotted gum creek,
Some bits shallow,
Some bits deep,
Full of tadpoles and
Tiny flies like stick people.

Then we found
Slippery Rock.
Mirragan, the giant tiger-cat and
Gurangatch, half-snake, half-fish struggled there,
Fighting so hard they made the rock
Slimy, slippery and smooth.

The place in the story,
Amazing to see it for real.

I loved the way my young son had been touched by the place; to see him get dreamy about the landscape. I also enjoyed seeing him learning from Philip, being taught how to use tools and how easy it is to build and fix things; to use your hands. He was growing up inquisitive and thoughtful, and I was certain the bush block had played a role in this. My only regret was about his brother, Joe, four years younger. The house was now pretty much finished and Joe had not really had the chance to play a part in its construction.

It was just the luck of the draw, of course, life's lottery. Next time he should arrange to be born a few years earlier.

TEN

The house was now there to be enjoyed. For me it was a thrill just to walk through the door. Each time we arrived for a weekend I'd think, 'We did this.' Even turning on the tap in the bathroom gave me a surge of joy. When visitors came I'd boss them into having a shower, whether they wanted one or not. My tone of voice suggested I was offering some sort of exotic experience, like a bath in ass's milk. 'You should try the *shower*,' I'd say, as if I was breaking news of some new luxurious device.

Before they could have a wash, I would insist on describing the shower's operation, showing them the solar panel and how it connected to the battery, then how the battery connected to the 12-volt pump, and, if they wouldn't mind coming outside, they could see the LPG cylinder and how it supplied fuel to heat the water.

Just how interesting can an LPG cylinder be? According to me: very. This was not a shower; it was a triumph of hope over adversity.

The place lacked electricity but this was one of its advantages. There were no televisions, no phones, no computer games. We cooked dinner mainly on the fireplace. We even overcame the early problem of incinerated meat. An opposite problem arose: I had formed the view that meat should be served rare. Very rare.

Philip: 'The bloody thing is still mooing.'

Me: 'Fuck off, it's perfect.'

Philip: 'You just held a match under it. That's your version of cooking.'

Me. 'Shut up.'

Philip: 'Who are you saying "Shut up" to — me or the meat?'

Me: 'The meat is perfect.'

Philip: 'Mate, when the chef has to shoosh the meat, you know it's undercooked.'

We read, talked, played charades. I installed a second solar panel, enough to run a record player, which I placed on the landing at the top of the stairs. I visited the Mittagong St Vincent de Paul and purchased an armful of '60s easy-listening records for 30 cents a go — *Hugo Winterhalter Goes...Continental*, *Mantovani's Golden Hits*, Bert Kaempfert's *Swinging Safari*. I ended up with 14 different versions of the 'Girl from Ipanema'. It was musical treacle flowing through the house. I christened

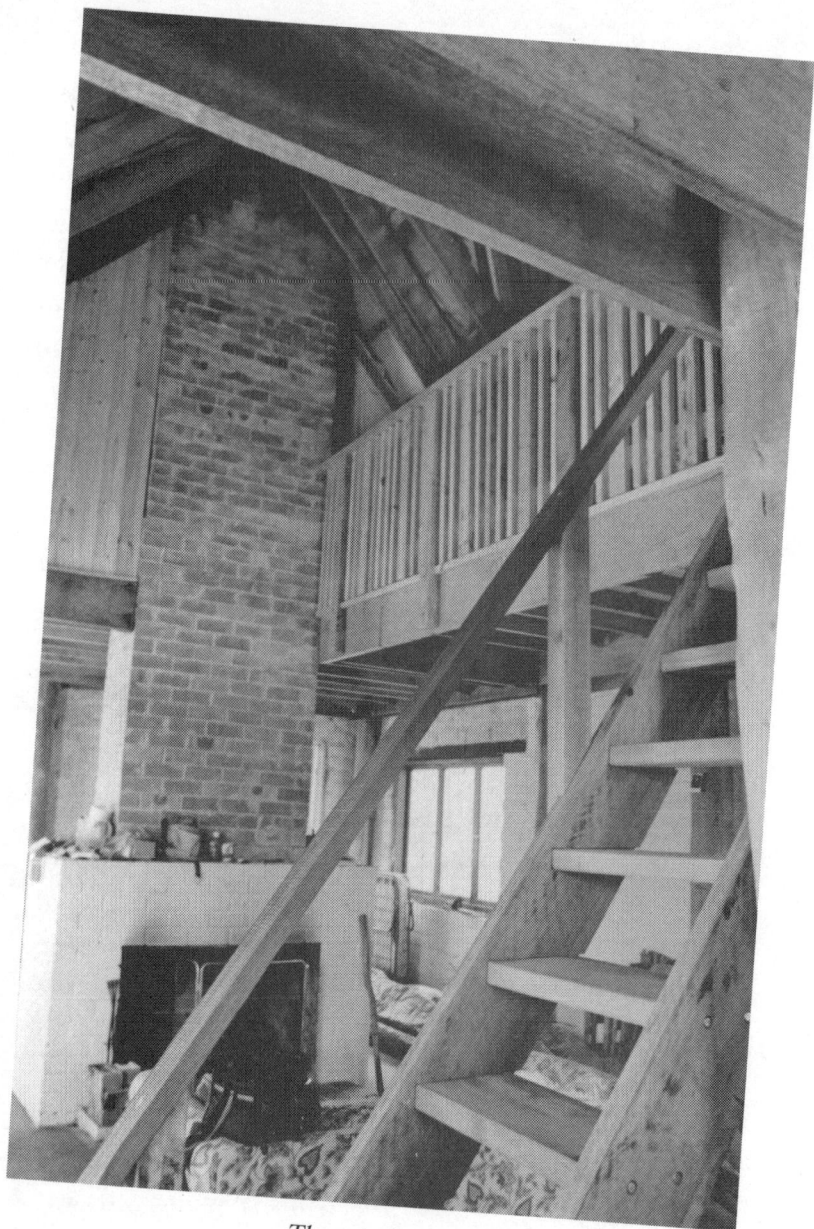

The stairs leading up to the 'Minstrels' Gallery'.

the area on the top of the stairs: it would be called the 'Minstrels' Gallery', as if Mantovani was up there in person serenading us.

The mudbrick, meanwhile, performed exactly as advertised: the building was cool in summer and warm in winter. On a windy and stormy day, rainwater might pelt the walls, but it never seemed to do any damage. Pliny had been proved right. The bricks also looked beautiful — a light tan colour which matched the landscape.

On the inside, we whitewashed the bricks. For the outside, the books had suggested various options: the modern practice was to paint them with watered-down Bondcrete, a plastic adhesive which would seal the bricks to moisture. The traditionalists preferred cowpats. You'd fill up a 44-gallon drum with cow dung, add water, leave to soak and then apply it to the walls. Apparently it was better than Bondcrete because it would 'allow the building to breathe'. Yes, but would it 'allow the inhabitants to breathe'? In the end we used neither method, and left the outside surface untreated. That seemed to work fine.

After about a year, we installed an old oven, linked to an LPG cylinder. The food was hardly fancy; we ate steak, potatoes, a box of Weet-Bix for breakfast. The weekends were full of simple pleasures — some food, a long walk, playing cards with the kids by the fire. As we drove up for the weekend, I developed a habit of describing the forthcoming menu to Debra, Dan and Joe. The plainer the tucker, the more I would bung it on.

'Tonight I'll be preparing a confit of potatoes,' I'd say as I steered the car up the highway. 'To the potatoes, I'll add a splash of cow's milk, gathered directly from the cow just days ago, mixed with some churned butter. This will then be dusted with a light mix of iodised salt and freshly ground black pepper.'

Dan, ten years old, would roll his eyes. 'Mum, he's just talking about mash.'

I'd ignore him. 'I intend serving the potato confit alongside a regional speciality — I have a local man who takes minced meat, bread-meal and some spices, and he encases them in a sort of tube.'

'Mum he's just talking about sausages.'

'These sausages — since that's the term you appear to prefer — will be grilled on a fire of fallen eucalypt branches, gathered by local young people hunting through nearby forests. Some lightly steamed green beans will be served alongside.'

There would be renewed groaning from Dan. 'Make him stop, Mum.'

This would leave me much encouraged. With the right amount of detail, my menu speech could take us from the outskirts of Sydney to halfway up the freeway.

'Dessert,' I'd continue after a break, 'has been sourced through a chocolate company called Cadbury's, which produces its wares from a site close to the Derwent River in historic Tasmania. Fresh bananas, imported from a plantation built on steep slopes in southern Queensland, will be available to diners in an informal smorgasbord arrangement.'

More groaning. Music to my ears. At this rate I could spin the menu out to the end of the freeway.

'For breakfast I have in mind some ears of wheat. These have been threshed, the grains flattened and toasted, and then pressed into a rectangular block. This dish will be served again with fresh cow's milk and a dusting of sugar, which we have sourced ...'

'Oh shut up, Dad.'

'Yeah,' Debra would agree, 'shut up.'

'Yeah, Dad, shut up,' squeaked Joe.

←

We went on long hikes through the bush. The kids loved the creek most of all — starting at what they still called Slippery Rock. Dan and Joe would clamber along the rocky banks, reporting back with tales of a goanna they'd spotted or of a new wombat hole.

We bought an archery set and, in a moment of madness, a cheap croquet set. We became experts in bush croquet, playing on what must have been the rockiest course in the world. The crumbling sheep pens were turned into a volleyball court by Dan: the net constructed of old chicken wire tied onto a rope slung between two poles, which he'd expertly cut from the bush.

During one game Joe broke his finger playing volleyball. I rushed him to Goulburn Base Hospital, where he was treated in a cubicle, slotted between two maximum-security prisoners from the local jail, each with their own armed entourage.

Joe, whispering: 'What do you think he's in for, Dad?'

Me, keen to please: 'Murder. With that many guards it would have to be murder.'

From then on Joe always seemed to play volleyball with unreasonable gusto, as if hoping to re-break the finger and get to again see his pals at Goulburn casualty.

Occasionally someone would suggest a new building project — but nothing ever happened. It was a blessed relief to be spared the mud, the pain, the sawing and the farting. It was wonderful not to work yourself to death every time you walked through the gate. This was the house's latest incarnation: somewhere to come and do nothing.

I was beginning to realise how the role of the house kept changing to match the stages of our lives. In the first few years, the place was all about friendship: the four owners would race up every weekend, sometimes with a gaggle of friends. Our pals, like us, were then in their mid-20s. They didn't yet have the responsibilities of kids and Saturday sport. They were happy to help make bricks — the women as enthusiastic as the men — or just lie about talking.

Then came children and things seemed to shift. Debra became less involved in the building. She would come up to the block but end up looking after Dan, or she'd volunteer to do the cooking. She would wonder aloud about the sexism that had crept into parts of our relationship after the arrival of our first child. Sometimes, exhausted by work and family, she'd elect to stay in town on the weekend.

For similar reasons, our friends also came less often, and for a while, the block became a place for Philip and me to escape and build — often just the two of us, working mad hours, drinking too much, amusing ourselves by talking bullshit.

Now even that had changed. The project was finished. Both Philip and I were busy at work. Philip had left his life in politics and become a journalist, ending up in radio. A few years later I made the same move. Bizarrely, we found ourselves working at the same station. He hosted the breakfast show while I hosted the drive-time show, so we saw each other at work. Without a project, Phil was also less keen to visit the block; it was the process of building he loved most of all.

The house now received only occasional visits, usually from Debra and me, accompanied by Dan and Joe. It was still important to us; a way of anchoring ourselves to this piece of beautiful bush and the house we'd created. Sometimes, in the city, I would lie awake at night thinking about it: I could make myself calm and happy just by summoning a mental image of some part of the block. The gum trees, shimmering as they had done on that first day we'd seen the place. Or the dam paddock full of kangaroos at dusk. Or the mud house itself, sitting on its pad of earth, silhouetted against the high blue sky.

Debra was still writing plays. One of them, *Gary's House*, was about a group of no-hopers building a house in the bush. I wonder how she got that idea? It was theatrically unusual, asking the actors to build a house on stage during the course of the play. In some productions they really went for it, the actors hauling around big bits of tin and cladding just as we had done. The characters, to be fair, were quite different from us; and the plot took them to a very different place emotionally. Still, plenty of the building techniques in the play were straight from the mud house.

The play was performed in Melbourne and other cities around Australia and made its way onto the NSW school drama syllabus. Later it was performed in translation in countries such as Japan and Denmark. I wondered what landscape they imagined, in Tokyo or Copenhagen, when they read the play's setting — 'a building site on a remote bush block'. I felt privileged to know exactly the picture that had been in Debra's head.

The land had now become a safety valve for Debra and me. We both had jobs in which we put ourselves up for judgement — me on the radio; her with her writing. We were constantly assessed by other people; sometimes complimented, sometimes found wanting. The world of Sydney could seem full of hierarchies, jealousies. It was important for us to hang onto the notion that none of this mattered as much as it might have seemed, and the mud house kept us grounded. It gave us something to hang onto in that storm of praise and criticism, success and rejection. There was something about the long, winding drive to the bush that made the world of the city seem small and distant. The troubles and tensions fell away with every hairpin bend; with every signpost urging you to 'sound horny on blind corners'. We'd slip through the rock tunnel at the start of the winding, dirty road and feel we were emerging into a different world. We would both notice that if we hadn't been up there for a few weeks we'd become tense and depressed, as if we were being denied some vitamin essential to our wellbeing. The mud house had again changed its role in our lives, and was giving us exactly what we needed.

The tunnel (blasted through rock in 1899) that marks the entrance to the magical kingdom, from where the city suddenly seems so small and disant.

The best fun was to take up friends, particularly friends from overseas. Up there, they could see kangaroos in the wild, stumble over wombat holes, and go for a swim in a country dam. 'You'll fall in love with the Aussie bush,' we'd promise as we bundled various visitors and exchange students into the car.

One weekend, we took up two friends from England, Matt and Julian. We were sitting inside the house having breakfast when a knock came on the door. It was Dr Richard Malik, a professor of vet science who raised cattle on a neighbouring block. He had a bull in his stockyards and was keen to perform a small operation.

'The bull is partly sedated, but I need a heavy man to help keep it under control,' said the prof. He seemed to be addressing his remarks to me. Presumably he had noted my girth from afar.

The operation on the bull seemed a great opportunity to give our visitors a real taste of rural life. We wandered down with the prof. Once we arrived at the yards we spotted the bull: it was lying on its side, eyes open, but its limbs lolling. The prof explained the nature of the operation. He intended to remove the bull's testicles. He wanted me to be astride its neck at the moment he made the cut.

I found it hard to chicken out, right there in front of my English friends. 'Are you sure this will be alright?' I asked as I gingerly placed myself atop the bull's neck. My voice, I noticed, was squeaking in a way that suggested he'd already tested out the operation on me.

'I'm pretty sure the dose will hold him,' the prof said calmly. 'But he may buck a bit when I make the incision. Just don't let him get his head up.'

Testicles suddenly seemed to be a dominant theme in my life. Only 24 hours earlier I'd been sitting in a Sydney medical centre having my own testicles examined by a doctor. Debra had become concerned when I complained about a slightly aching ball, and had ordered me to the doctor. The examination was going fine until the doctor confided that he really liked my radio show. This sort of compliment — regrettably rare — is usually most welcome. But not when the chap delivering the compliment is simultaneously giving one's left testicle a light squeeze.

I wondered what he was thinking. Presumably: 'No wonder he doesn't speak as deeply as John Laws.'

Back in the bush the bull shifted beneath me. I had my hands outstretched holding his large head to the ground. His eyes, a little glazed, stared balefully up at me.

'If only you knew what's about to happen,' I thought to myself.

It turned out the bull was owned by another neighbour, Tim, who was also there to help, holding one of the bull's legs. 'Are you sure we shouldn't have two people sitting on him?' I asked Tim. Tim thought this was a great idea.

I called over my friend Matt. At least it would give him something to put in his postcards home — even if the postcards were posted from Goulburn Base Hospital after his treatment for concussion consequent to being gored by a bull. Debra pushed our lightly-built companion forward and he clambered over the fence. I made a spot for him to sit, right there at the front on the dangerous end of the bull.

'No, no,' instructed the prof, pointing at me. 'The bigger man on the front, the lighter man behind.'

Doctors often say an excess 15 kilograms can increase your chance of death; I just hadn't realised that 'trampled by bull' was the agency by which this might be achieved.

I pressed down on the head. My friend spooned me from behind. We looked like two men having sex atop a partly stunned bull while the latter's balls were being removed. Surely, there was some shady corner of the internet where I could post these photos to considerable acclaim.

As I pushed down on the head, I thought about my own ball troubles. There was something that worried me about the doctor, in particular his enthusiasm for my radio show. On the odd occasion I meet someone who listens to me on the radio, they inevitably make the same pleasant remark: 'It's good to finally put a face to the voice.' I could only imagine the doctor had a similar thought as he prodded away: 'It's good to finally put a pair of knackers to the face.'

An incision is made; the blade slicing into the skin. No, not at the doctor's. Back in the bush now. The bull kicked and started to bellow. 'Stay calm,' said the prof. 'Push down harder.'

From her vantage point behind the fence, Debra was taking an interest in the proceedings.

'Normally you just castrate the young calves, don't you?' she asked Tim. 'How come you are doing the bull?'

'He didn't turn out as good as I'd hoped. He's a bit rubbish,' the grazier replied with a shrug.

Debra nodded as if she understood and believed the principle deserved a wider application among males. Braced against the bull's large head, I whispered in his ear, 'Mate, I didn't turn out as well as some people hoped. But this particular punishment ... I just hope it doesn't become the general rule.'

Somewhere, on the surface of the testicles, he'd located a suspicious lump. No, not the professor of vet science. The doctor. It's benign, he said, but probably the explanation for my aching ball. He'd do some tests but I shouldn't worry. Standing up from his task, he shook my hand vigorously and said he was really looking forward to next week's edition of the radio show. I made a mental note to speak more deeply.

Back in the bush the vet sliced. The bull kicked, snorted, tried to stand and then relaxed. Suddenly all was still. The balls were gone. The deed was done. My friend and I hopped off and climbed gingerly over the fence. We spent the rest of the day sitting neatly, our knees pressed protectively together.

Sometimes it's tough being male.

Back in Sydney, Phil left our radio station to join the opposition. He and I ended up, again bizarrely, in the same time slot on competing stations — battling for ratings. Debra wrote several more plays and had a hit with one of them — *Mr Bailey's Minder*. For once I couldn't covet the windfall and translate the money into building materials. That project was finished. The children were growing older. We'd come to the end of something.

ELEVEN

In December 2003 we were on a family holiday in Greece, puffing up the trail through the ruins of Delphi Joe was 11, about to turn 12; his elder brother was 15. It was a fantastical place, cradled by mountains, full of remains from two and a half thousand years ago. Up high there were the ruins of an athletic stadium. Joe and Dan raced each other on the running track until they were dizzy and breathless. On the walk back down, Joe kept stopping to examine the half-collapsed stonework. It had been weathered down over two and half millennia, but the method of construction was instantly apparent. Rocks had been gathered, selected, and placed atop each other, a simple mortar holding them together. There was something about the construction which made even a child realise that building was easy — that anyone can build something.

Joe had spent plenty of time at the mud house but never as a builder. Now, on the track at Delphi, he stood back, looked at the ancient stonework and connected it with our homemade house.

'You know,' he said, 'we could build something new up at the bush. We could use a rock method just like this. It would be so easy. You just collect the rocks and go from there. I could draw up a plan.'

That night in the hotel he drew the first of what would be many plans. Joe's new building would be of rock, mortared together in the Greek way. It would be a one-room building, at right angles to the house we'd already built. It would feature a billiard table, or at the very least a ping-pong table. Down one end there would be a bar serving various refreshments.

Joe lay on the floor of the hotel room, stretched out on his stomach. He drew the sketch carefully — marking the position of the bar, the bar stools, even the couch that would sit over by the wood heater. He then drew a front-on view, marking in the door and the windows. He indicated the placement of a small hot plate beside the bar, on which the bartender — that was him — would prepare snacks and hot drinks.

'As soon as we get back home,' he said to no one in particular, 'we'll get started on this.'

He was only 11, of course. As I watched him daydream, I wondered how long his enthusiasm would last. Should I just humour him and let him enjoy the fantasy of building a place — knowing that it will never happen in practice?

The next day I saw him purloining a beer coaster from one of the Greek cafes, slipping it into his coat pocket. He ordered Dan to do the same.

'I've started a collection of beer mats,' he explained to his brother. 'I'm going to use them to decorate the walls of the new building.'

He'd also decided on a name for the place: 'The Delphi Bar'.

←

Once we arrived back in Australia, Joe couldn't talk of anything else. Part of me felt weary at the thought of a new project. Most of the hard slog of the house had been done when we were hovering around the age of 30. Now we were all in our mid-40s. My body, in particular, felt decidedly dicky. I was starting to develop arthritis in my left foot and left hand; my left knee and left hip were not so good either. Naturally, it was my left ball that had been a bit achy.

I found it strange that all my problems were limited to the left side. The right half of my body was still fine. On one side I was an ultra-fit 19-year-old; on the other side, I was a clapped-out 90-year-old. I was like *The Picture of Dorian Grey*, just all in the one body.

Yet I also knew this was an opportunity. Joe was opening a door to me. The word 'father' is a verb as well as a noun. It requires doing and not just being. As my son clambered into adolescence, we'd have a project to work on together. Despite everything — my aching back, my aching hip and my aching ball — how could I say anything other than 'yes'?

Joe wanted to build from stone, but over a few months I talked him around to mudbrick. I was worried that stone might defeat us: it's heavier than mud, and a less forgiving medium when it comes to construction involving idiots.

Joe started to work up his design — basing it on the proportions of the golden mean (a second contribution from Pythagoras). The idea is there's a perfect ratio of length, depth and height to a building, and the elements within the building, all of which can be expressed in a mathematical constant, approximately 1.6180339887. Joe had apparently learnt this at school, during a lesson in ancient history. Having built the first place under instruction from Pliny and Sisyphus, I found it hard to deny him his own flourish.

I kept quizzing Joe about his commitment to the project, much as one might question a child before buying a pet. Already I knew he was a boy of furious but sometimes short-lived enthusiasms. He'd wake up one morning and suddenly have a passion for building a guitar from scratch. Or installing a fish pond. Or building a home recording studio using nothing but egg cartons and a $12 microphone. He'd convince everyone that his new hobby was a lifelong passion; that he was suddenly involved in a transformative crusade that required immediate action.

He had a gift for certainty that reminded me of Philip. He'd put his case so compellingly — 'We need to build a table for the record player at the bush house' — that I'd find myself coaxed into the car at 9.30 on a Saturday morning to go in search of the urgently required materials. Only when I was halfway there would I recall that we'd had a similar call to arms only the week before — 'I want to build a Roman catapult' — resulting in just the same frenzied activity.

We'd buy or borrow the materials and then the passion would take hold, with Joe spreading signs of the new hobby throughout the house. He was like the armies of Rome: every day would bring the colonisation of a new region. The manufacture of a single guitar would consume every flat surface in the house. Joe was a blizzard that filled every space; an invading army that left the fields salted and the buildings burnt. During these times, Debra and I would live like mice, searching the house for small gaps in which we could nestle. Occasionally I'd order him to clean it all up. He'd look up with a cheery smile. 'That's fine,' he'd say happily. 'I'll do it in a second.'

People complain about sulky, monosyllabic teenagers but the chatty, friendly ones may be worse.

Joe, like most young people, had his own working definition of the time period known as 'a second'. He used it to mean: 'tomorrow, next week or most likely never'. He could have secured a position with Telstra, considering the lack of accuracy with which he predicted a job's completion.

His work, though, was beautiful. He'd calmly learn the skills required for his current passion and put in days of effort. And then, just hours away from the objective being achieved, the obsession would pass as suddenly as it had arrived. The house was full of almost completed guitars, nearly finished scale models of medieval weapons, sound baffles that were one egg carton short.

It made me worry. Did he understand the timescale of the building he was proposing? By now six months had passed, but he was still only 12. Did he understand that it might take until he was 17 or 18 for his building to be finished? Was he sure that this time he'd stick with something until it was entirely done?

Oh, yes, he was sure. He would stick with it all the way.

←

Another thing: I was keen that my second child wouldn't miss out on things that Dan had enjoyed. With a second child there's always a temptation to let your attention wander.

For the first child nothing is too much trouble. With the first child, bedtime involves enthusiastic readings from *Chicken Little* and *The Very Hungry Caterpillar*, embellished with the use of funny voices. You read as if the child's whole future is dependent on the number of hours you invest. You read until the kid begs for mercy. 'Daddy, I just want to go to sleep,' the poor mite sobs. 'I don't care if the caterpillar is still hungry.'

With the second child, you're reading the same books and frankly you're sick of the characters. The caterpillar's constant consumption of leaf matter has lost its allure. The thrill is gone. As for Chicken Little, once you know the sky doesn't fall in, the character seems shrill, panicky, even a little shallow. Who needs to spend this much time with neurotic poultry?

You start fake yawning, hoping the child will catch a yawn and fall asleep. More treacherous still, you secretly turn over two or three pages at a time, skipping whole chunks of plot. In extreme cases, you jump from halfway through the caterpillar's travails to a tacked-on 'and so he lived happily ever after'.

Surely they notice? Surely it must affect them? Is this why second children are generally a little wilder, a little more lateral in their thinking? Every time you skipped a whole chunk of *The Very Hungry Caterpillar*, did they internalise the anarchic notion that life is capricious, unpredictable and all too brief? Is this why they are more likely to be artists, professional surfers, high-risk rock climbers?

It's not only the reading. With the first child, TV shows are thoroughly monitored, soft drink is banned and homework times are enforced. By the second child, anything goes. It's like a prison in which the guards have become very, very lax. The guards are lying around, scratching their bellies, the prison gates swinging open. About 6pm, they distribute pizza menus and invite the inmates over for a Johnny Cash concert.

And then there are the photos. The first born is documented every second. It's like being under ASIO surveillance. There are whole photo albums dedicated to the time between two months and three months of age, a time during which their appearance changes from blob to slightly larger blob. By contrast, the second has no archive. He's Trotsky during the Stalin years, his very image scrubbed from the record. 'Of course, you're in the family photo album,' you assure your child. 'Look at the photo of the dog. I'm almost positive that's your foot in the background.'

This lack of photos was a reality for Joe. I was determined that the bush house would be different: if he wanted to build, just as Dan had done, he would have the chance.

←

Meanwhile, Joe kept working on his plan, while I gently questioned the size of the project. He was resolute. He again pledged he would see it through to the end. I didn't entirely believe him, of course, but the idea of building something new was beginning to take hold. It was a virus introduced by Joe, but a contagious one. I tentatively rang Philip. I had told him already about Joe's grand plan, but not as a solid idea. This time I did, explaining the size of the project — a room maybe half the size of the existing building — and the cost in money and time.

'I want to do this for Joe's sake,' I said. 'You shouldn't feel like you are required to sign up.'

There was no pause on Phil's side; just a tone of genuine excitement. 'It's a great idea. I'd love to get back up there building.' The contagion was spreading. It looked like the old team was back in business.

The design was settled over the next few months and then checked over by an engineer. This time we would have a concrete slab instead of footings, but otherwise the plan was quite similar to the first building — a strong wooden frame, built to the proportions of the golden mean; a tin roof over a large vaulted ceiling; and mudbricks filling in the walls. How many mudbricks? Philip did a calculation — about 2000 should do it. Minus the 50 we still had left over from last time.

Why exactly had I agreed to this? The whole left side of my body throbbed with anticipatory pain.

TWELVE

I was back at the mud pits, the wretched sun-baked mud pits of Wombeyan; that godless plain where the sun blazes down and grown men weep for the want of shade. The plateau of pain. The land of relentless effort. OK, I exaggerate, but not by much. At my feet were the wooden moulds we used last time we made bricks. To my right, a pile of old tools — a tangle of picks and shovels. The first time I made bricks here I was 26 years old, with no kids, early into my first job. This time I was closer to 50, a little out of condition, my left knee throbbing. Most dispiriting of all: I knew exactly what I was getting myself into. Standing with me were two 14-year-old boys — my son Joe and his mate, Ben. My older son, Dan, was now 18: that's how old I was. I had an adult son.

It was October school holidays, 7.30 in the morning, and already the air temperature was beginning to rise.

Within a few hours it would be baking hot; the air humming with heat. All three of us were wearing old clothes, topped off with wide-brimmed straw hats. We looked like a down-on-its-luck mariachi band.

Joe put the question: 'How many bricks did you and Phil make in a day?'

I plucked a largish figure. 'Some days we managed three pits. Ninety or 95 bricks. But that's a big ask.'

'I reckon we can do more,' bragged Joe.

'Yeah,' chimed Ben. 'Ninety-five doesn't sound much.'

I permitted myself a mocking laugh. 'Let's see if you still feel that way by lunchtime'.

Joe had been waiting for this moment since that hillside in Greece. For two and a half years, we had been unable to pass by a pub without him ordering me inside to steal some beer coasters. Friends on overseas trips had been given similar orders. His plans for The Delphi Bar

Ben, me and Joe ... the mudbrick squad.

called for a glass-topped ledge all along one wall, with the exotic coasters on display beneath the glass. He would also discuss, in some detail, the size of the billiard table we would need to buy, and the complexities of providing lighting for the table using a 12-volt solar system. On the way home from school, he regularly trawled the local St Vincent de Paul looking for useful stuff. One day he came home with two black waistcoats.

'Look what I found — $4 each. Perfect for the waiters to wear when serving drinks at The Delphi Bar.'

'You don't think you're getting ahead of yourself?' I asked him at the time. 'Maybe we should make the bricks, before we design the uniforms for the staff.'

This may sound a little grouchy, but Joe's enthusiasm cannot be dented; he would have bought the polish for the front door handle if I'd let him. Already he had a collection of foreign beer bottles, purloined from my friends, to display on a shelf above the bar. Ben had also been delegated to collect bottles — leaping into action whenever his father opened a Singha or a Grolsch.

Ben had been Joe's friend since they were both five, together in kindergarten at the local school. Joe had spent months convincing Ben of the brilliance of The Delphi Bar project. Ben had agreed to help — giving over eight days of his school holidays to the relentless task of making mudbricks, all the while covered in flies and standing in blazing heat. Not since Tom Sawyer conned the neighbourhood kids into painting Aunt Polly's fence had such an unlikely agreement been achieved.

As we stood in the dewy grass, I explained some of the finer details of brick making — how the boys would have to push the mud down into the wooden mould; how the moulds needed to be washed after every few bricks so the corners didn't clog with old mud.

What a moment it was. Me — the ballet-dancing boy who couldn't hold a hammer — had become a teacher of ancient male skills, passing on building techniques to these two young men. Here, surely, was the point of transcendence: their youthful faces looking up, eager for instruction; my quiet yet impressive tutelage ...

Of course, it didn't work out like that. The boys were not really listening. They just wanted to get started. They wanted to beat the record set by Philip and me. They want to prove how *soft* we were.

I gave up the lesson and we started making our first pit of mud. Shovelling in the dirt, we then chucked in the usual additions: a handful of straw, a benediction of cement and a few buckets of water. Together we worked the mixture — pushing and prodding with our various shovels and hoes.

The boys thought the word 'hoe' was hilarious. 'Can I borrow your hoe, please?' I asked one of them, and they both laughed so hard I thought they might well have died. Remember, they were 14.

We decided the boys would make the bricks while I tried to keep the mud up to them — shovelling it out of the pit into a wheelbarrow, then heaving the wheelbarrow up to where they were working. I gave the mud a final mix. If it's too dry, the bricks tend to crumble; if it's too sloppy the mix slumps once you take off the mould, the edges bowing outwards. This mix seemed about right.

I filled up the barrow and pushed it up towards the flat bit of land. The boys had set up sheets of plywood, on top of which they placed the moulds. I dolloped a couple of big shovel loads of mud into each mould and it hit the plywood with a wet squish. The boys crouched over their work — pushing the mud into the corners with their fingers, just as Debra and Gillian had done on that first day 21 years before. They splashed a handful of water onto their brick mixture, then used a flat stick to create a neat, level top. They each wriggled their moulds up and off, leaving two bricks to dry on the ground.

Joe and Ben stood and admired their work. The bricks were perfect. 'Next,' yelled Joe, and we were off and running again. The boys worked incredibly fast, racing each other.

'Third brick finished. What about you?' inquired Joe.

'I'm on the fourth,' replied Ben. 'But I've run out of mud.'

They enjoyed the sight of me hurrying to keep up. I was shovelling out the pit I'd already made, while trying to create a second pit so there'd be no break in proceedings. I charged up the hill with the barrow, charged back down, hurled some dirt in a second pit, refilled the barrow with mud from the first pit, then fetched water from the dam. I donkeyed the water up to the second pit and started mixing. After a while, I paused very briefly to stretch my back.

'More mud!' shouted Joe, disturbed at the sight of his father momentarily still.

'Yeah, it's not a holiday camp,' agreed Ben.

Ben, whom I'd known since he was five, had always been exceedingly polite and kind, yet within minutes of arriving on a worksite, he had intuitively discovered the need to deliver a rich steam of abusive banter.

'We need more mud,' Joe repeated. 'What are you doing?'

'Probably spending time with his hoe,' quipped Ben.

They both fell about laughing. It was possibly the funniest thing said by any human being at any time in human history. They were breathless with their own Wildean wit. They were 14.

We used up the contents of the first pit by 10.30; a second pit by noon. The boys had made 79 bricks. I felt like booking into a rest home for much of the next decade.

Joe slapped aside a few flies. He was enjoying the moment. 'So, a whole day to make 95 bricks. And we've made ... what was that figure again, Ben?'

'It's 79. So far, 79.'

'And what time is it, Dad?'

'It's noon.'

'Really? It's only noon?' said Joe, affecting a peachy-keen surprise. 'Because it looks like the old record of 95 bricks is not going to stand for long. We'll overtake it by about 2pm, don't you think, Ben?'

'Well, Joe, either that, or a bit before,' chimed Ben.

Really they were both quite obnoxious. On the other hand, they had made what we mudbrick makers describe as a shitload of bricks.

We headed up to the house to take a lunch break. I decided not to tell them the truth about the 95 bricks, and how rarely even that small figure had been achieved. It's true we eventually made them that quickly — but only after about a year in which we averaged about 65 bricks a day.

As usual with the mud house, it was all due to a misguided method. When we first started making bricks, we used the technique described earlier, in which we removed all the stones, passing every shovel load of dirt through a chicken-wire mesh. It was basically Pliny's idea, and in retrospect suited a society featuring institutionalised slavery. It was fantastically laborious and left the site dotted with middens of small stones, like strange sculptures. Over the course of two years, we made about 3000 bricks using this method, at which point we asked the obvious question: 'Do we really need to remove all the stones?'

If we shovelled the dirt straight into the pit, the larger stones could be plucked out at the last minute, while you were crouched down pushing the mud into the mould. And if a few smaller stones ended up embedded within the brick, who cares? We gave it a try. The bricks turned out to be just as good. We could easily make 95 a day. The only disappointment: we had only about 500 still to make. If we had questioned our method earlier, we could have knocked about four months off our timetable.

It was another costly mistake. Maybe it was good we now had a second shot at building.

By the end of lunch the brick field was incredibly hot. The boys barked at me for mud as they punched out the bricks — chanting out the numbers as they got up towards 95. I loved their fierce determination; their focused aggression. Maybe this is why young men are hungry for practical projects; it's a way of channelling their competitive, restless energy. They achieved their 95th brick just before 2pm, gave a cheer, and allowed themselves 20 minutes of lolling in the shade of the ute, slurping water. Then they were back into it, shouting abuse at the poor mud man for failing to keep up supply.

By 5.30pm I was whimpering piteously. I still felt like The-Picture-of-Dorian-Gray-But-All-In-One-Person.

My right side felt fine, but my left knee and left hip were feeling so ancient they expected a telegram from the Queen. The boys graciously acceded to my request to stop work. By this time, they had made 105 bricks, which now sat slowly drying in long rows on the flatter parts of the paddock. We all staggered back to the house. I scrubbed off the mud in the shower, then poured myself a large beaker of red wine. Another difference with the past: it was bottled stuff this time; better than the 25-cent shiraz from the bladder. I cooked us dinner, after which the boys — seemingly unbowed by their labours — demanded a few rounds of charades. I did my best with

Joe and Ben with their bricks, ready for use in The Delphi Bar.

my performance, despite listing to the left, like the Hunchback of Notre Dame. By 9.30pm, we were all asleep.

Each day we made more bricks: 110 on day two; 117 on day three; 119 on day four. The totals were amazing but still short of the insane targets which the boys set for themselves each morning.

'Let's make 200,' crowed Joe.

'That's nothing. What about 250,' countered Ben.

It was like an insane game of poker, in which both sides were bidding up their shared pain.

Along the way, we came up with other innovations. The books tell you to make the bricks on sheets of old plywood; but we discovered they take longer to dry that way. The ply stops the water escaping. We started instead to whack the wooden mould on a bit of bare earth.

We also discovered the mud is easier to handle if it's been left to soak for a while. Whenever I had the chance, I'd make an extra pit before lunch, or at the end of the day, to maximise this soaking time.

By day five, my body hummed with pain. The term 'rotator cuff injury' was no longer an obscure medical notion; it spoke of a part of my body that was insistently begging for mercy. Since I shovelled with my right arm, for once I had an injury on that side of my body. Hurrah! At long last my right side knew what my left side had been going through.

I also spent most of my time with my eyes lowered towards the ground — watching my feet as I stumbled wearily up the hill; or staring down into the pit as I mixed the mud. I discovered my eyelids were badly sunburnt. It was the one place I hadn't applied sun block.

But day six and we were back at it. The boys never complained. They just worked. They were dogged and scoffed whenever I took a break.

Joe: 'Bit tired, are we?'

Ben: 'Poor old man looks tired out.'

Joe: 'Maybe you need to take another holiday with your hoe.'

As the bricks dried we would turn them up on their long sides. A day later we would shift them again, standing each upright on its short end. Then, another day on, we'd carry them to the back of the ute — one at a time, since they were 15 kilos each — and then I'd drive them up to the building site.

We took two days off at the end to allow the last of the bricks to dry, so they could all be stacked safely under tin, ready for use. That brought it to eight days, including drying, by which time we had made 649 bricks — close to a third of the number we'd need. The boys posed for photos behind the huge pile of stacked bricks ready for use in The Delphi Bar.

I asked Ben if he'd enjoyed his holiday — a holiday of 10-hour work days, of flies, mud and pain. 'Yeah,' he enthused with apparent sincerity. 'It was fun.'

←

Life was shifting again. Dan was about to leave home — heading off to university. As the hour ticked closer I was becoming a little anxious. I still had so many things to teach him. I wanted to tell him not to get in a car with drunk people. I needed to explain about snakes and long grass. And how you must defrost a frozen chicken before cooking it.

What had I been doing for these past 18 years that I'd failed to teach him this stuff? I remembered how gormless I was at 18, before the experiences of the bush house, among other things, had taught me about the world. Dan was presumably ignorant in similar ways. I considered packing it all into one 10-hour lesson. 'This, son, is how to operate a food processor.' 'The easiest way of putting a doona in its cover is to first turn the cover inside out.' 'It is dangerous to leave oil heating unattended on the stove top — notice how, after a given amount of time, it bursts into flames.'

Dan was packing up his room, ready to move his life down to Canberra. He'd decided — no pressure from his parents — to go to ANU, the place where Debra and I had met. I watched him as he marched by, carrying his stuff to the car. Each time he passed by me I spouted another helpful piece of information.

'If you see a hole in the ground it could be a funnel-web's nest, so no way should you put your finger into it.'

'Mayonnaise is OK in the cupboard until you open the jar. At that point it must be refrigerated.'

'The emu is a dangerous bird. Don't be fooled into thinking they are friendly, because they certainly aren't.'

Dan flashed me a look of pity. 'Exactly how do you think I survived up until this point?'

I saw he was trying to put me off, but also knew this was my last chance. At least, during his time at the block, he'd learnt a little about bush cooking and bush building. But I needed to tell him about so much more.

'Establish a file for any bank statements or warranties you may wish to keep.'

'Electrical problems should always be left to a professional.'

'Watch out for small, yappy dogs; they don't look it, but they can be even more vicious than the big ones.'

As Dan gathered his possessions, Debra was overcome by a surge of maternal hormones. She was now attempting to press into his hands anything that was not nailed down. Dan, never a materialist, was fighting her off.

'It's fine,' he said. 'I really don't need anything at all.'

Undeterred, Debra roamed the house, offering him all my best stuff. 'What about Dad's penknife?' she said. 'That could be useful.'

Or pausing at my desk: 'He doesn't use his briefcase much — would you like it?'

Or thinking outside the square: 'Maybe you should take up carpentry. Dad's just bought this really good circular saw. You could take it down and set it up in your room. He only uses it every now and then.'

It was like watching a demented salesman at Harvey Norman: 'Everything must go. No interest. Free steak knives. No need to pay.'

I wished she would just control herself and calm down. I still needed a moment to warn the boy about mosquitoes and the dangers of Ross River fever.

←

It took another year to make all the bricks for The Delphi Bar. Sometimes Joe brought a friend; at other times, it was back to the two couples — Philip and Diana, Debra and me. Often Dan would join in, driving up with a pal from university. Dan was a terrific brick maker, full of Joe's zeal and the same delight in verbally abusing his father.

'Come on, old man; pick it up a little. We're not in the retirement home yet.'

If he wasn't careful, I'd keep any future warnings about emus, snakes and defrosted chickens to myself. I also had a particularly pertinent point to make about the dangers of undercooked pork.

It was hard, even with Dan's help, to make much progress on occasional weekends. Partly that was because the bricks needed to dry for a day or two before they could be safely stacked. One Saturday there were five of us working — the two couples and Joe. We made 148 bricks, but then there was a crack of thunder and it started to rain. The bricks were too wet to carry; too wet

Joe and Dan mixing mud mortar.

even to nurse under temporary shelter. I was forced to leave them in the field.

I spent most of the night awake, listening to the rain and estimating its likely impact. By morning all the bricks were ruined. A week or two later we made another 150 bricks — Philip urging the team on with promises of medals, trophies or at least a glass of red. Then, late on Saturday afternoon, the sky darkened and again it rained. And again all the bricks were ruined.

Debra was not happy. For years we'd tried to find a name for this block of land but had never come up with anything suitable. 'Finally I've got it,' she said, as she hopped back in the car for the trip home. 'We'll call it Pissing Downs.'

Our spirits were dented and we found ourselves avoiding the block for nearly two months. Just after

Christmas we had another burst of effort — three days of ferocious brick making. By the middle of the week, we had hundreds of bricks drying in the field. Philip drove Debra and Joe back to Sydney while I stayed on to let the bricks dry for a day or two and then move them to safety.

I watched Phil's car beetle off down the road and for a moment enjoyed the solitude; the lazy time in which you finally have no work to do. Then I heard a crack of thunder and felt the first drops of rain. I rushed down to the field and desperately started carrying the still damp bricks up the hill to my ute. The storm built up, the sky roaring and flashing. I didn't want to be hit by lightning but I was determined to save our days of labour. I tramped up the hill with another precious brick, imagining the headline that would follow my death from lightning strike: 'Man Dies in Vain Bid to Save Mudbrick'.

I filled the ute with bricks then gingerly drove up towards the building site. With the rain starting to ease, I took my time unstacking the bricks. Maybe they would be OK after all.

It was about 5.30pm, the sky still dark with occasional cracks of thunder. I spotted a small car nosing its way up the dirt road towards our block. It was rare to see a car up here, especially one I didn't recognise. The car drove past the gate, stopped and then reversed. A tall man in his late 30s hopped out of the vehicle and came running up the drive. When he spoke I heard an American accent.

'There's a tree hit by lightning down on the main road. It's started a fire. I thought I should tell someone.'

I was still focused on my bricks. I prefer to handle my crises one at a time. A fire, though, takes priority. I grabbed the chainsaw and a couple of long-handled shovels. We jumped in the man's small car and headed back down the road. As we drove he explained he was an American tourist, who had only landed in the country a day ago.

'How did you end up here?'

'That's a long story.'

By the time we arrived at the main road, the crew from the Rural Fire Service was already on the scene. The trunk of an old gum tree was burning but they had things under control. Then the rain started belting down once again.

I asked the American to drive me back so I could move more bricks and he offered his help. I declined — 'the work is too dirty' — but he insisted. For the next two hours, we worked like rescue workers in a flood, moving bricks from the paddock up to the building site. By 8pm, we'd moved the last one. It was already dark and we were covered from head to toe in mud. What else could I do but invite him to stay the night?

We both took showers and I cooked us dinner. Finally he told me his story. He was from Utah, a non-observant Mormon, whose marriage had just broken up. He had come to Australia to get away and think about his wife and child. At the airport he'd hired a car but had refused the offer of a map. At every crossroads he met he just went the way that looked best — out of the airport, onto the M5 tollway, then the Hume, on a whim taking the turn-off to Mittagong, then the fork to Berrima, then the turn to the Wombeyan Caves. An hour up the dirt road, he saw the fire, took the nearest side road to find help, and stumbled onto me. Then helped save 200 bricks.

His name was Erin, and he left the next morning, committed to a journey on which he'd just take a chance at every crossroads. It was an unusual holiday technique, but probably left *Lonely Planet* for dead. It was also proof that the mountains were losing none of their power in terms of attracting the mad, the passionate and the unconventional.

Granny Lang would be pleased.

THIRTEEN

We'd now made close to 2000 bricks, all of them stacked beneath sheets of old tin. It was time to start building a whole new frame. Philip, acting as quantity surveyor, ordered a big load of timber — mostly the thick uprights that would hold up the roof. After much discussion we'd also decided to invest in a generator; instead of the hours of handsawing and hand-drilling that went into the first building, this time we'd use power tools. Philip was keen about the new project, but felt that power tools might be an acceptable innovation, considering our advanced ages.

It was 7am on a misty winter morning when I turned on the new generator for the first time and tentatively pulled the starting cord. It had cost nearly $2000, but I never expect these things to work; there's always a problem. Not this time. The generator smoothly chugged into life. Philip plugged in a circular saw and pressed the trigger. The blade spun. It was a miracle. Two hundred and fifty years after the Industrial Revolution, power tools had finally arrived at Wombeyan.

The plan for the building was still the one dreamt up by Joe, lying on the floor of the hotel room in Delphi. It was a rectangle 10 metres by 6 metres, with a front door flanked on each side by two windows. The roof would be held up by 14 hardwood posts, each of them 15 centimetres square. Around the bottom we'd have a heavy skirting board, inset into the bottom of each post. And around the top a perimeter beam, similarly inset. Across the top, some wooden ties would create a stable rectangular box, on top of which we could build the roof structure. The walls, of course, would be mudbrick.

First we had to trim each post to size, cutting rebates on both ends to fit the skirting board and the perimeter beam. In the old building this would have taken days, battling away with handsaws. This time we cut the posts to length with a single swipe of the circular saw. The rebates took a little more effort, but we made the most of the power saw — setting the blade to the right depth we made multiple crosscuts, then chopped out the unwanted wood using a chisel and hammer.

By the end of the first day we had all the posts prepared. Day two we started putting the frame up, and — oh delight — again discovered that power tools are quite useful. The power drill bores a hole in a couple of seconds. Few builders would experience such pleasure through use of an electric drill. It's a sensation only

The Industrial Revolution finally arrives at
Wombeyan — two and a half centuries late.

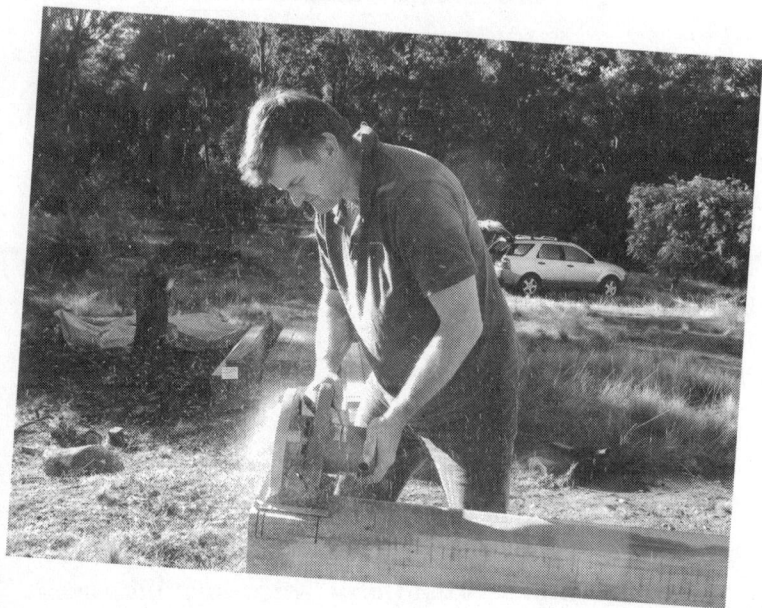

available to those who have previously endured 10 years
drilling into hardwood with a brace and bit.

With each use of the drill we purred with delight.
This was what it must have been like when the canal-
building navvies of Manchester first experienced the joy
of the steam shovel; when the timber-cutters of Canada
were first handed a chainsaw. I pressed down the trigger
and felt like James Watt turning on his invention for the
first time. The generator purred in response and the hole
was instantly drilled. Why didn't we buy a generator first
time round? Oh, that's right, we didn't have the $2000
spare cash.

Plus we were idiots.

◂—

There was one thing better than the power tools. We
were back on the worksite, sharing jokes and insults as
we went.

Him to me: 'You bludger, why don't you try lifting it?'

Or me to him: 'Can't quite reach that nail? Why don't
you let a bloke who is more than four foot tall have
a try?'

As usual, the jokes weren't particularly funny. They
were just careless insults knocked together on the go, but
they provided the ebb and flow of the day.

We carried each post into position. Phil put his end
on the ground and then I hinged it upwards with a grunt
of effort.

More bad jokes: 'Where did you get this stuff?' I asked. 'It's much heavier timber than the stuff we were using 20 years ago.'

It started raining but we worked on. We were determined to have the uprights in by the end of the weekend. Phil — through some promotional deal at the local hardware store — had a fabulous new rain-jacket, manufactured by the people who make Stihl chainsaws. Emblazoned on the chest were the words 'Stihl Farm Boss'. I was wearing a light lady's rain-jacket, three sizes too small, with a busted zip. I decided mine should be labelled the 'Stihl Indentured Slave'.

It was true that Philip still did more of the planning work and the jobs that required real skill, and I was the hired help of the operation; lifting, sweeping, bolting off. It was now nearly 30 years since we had met. We had both become greyer, yet the old differences between us remained: Philip charging into the task; me mentally reviewing each of Philip's decisions. 'We don't want another visit from Fuck-up Phil,' I would say sweetly as I checked his sums.

'Go fuck yourself,' he would reply, just as sweetly.

Certainly, as we worked we swore like crazy. I don't advocate the f-word in polite society, but out there it was a necessity. On a building site, the f-word is an aid to exertion. As I lifted each post into place, I needed to summon my resources with a bit of verbal fire power. There's also something perfect about the word 'f---' and its explosive sound: the way the bottom lip curls behind the teeth, building up the pressure like a slingshot, before flinging the word forward into the world. Try that with 'holy moly'. In building a house, the f-words are as crucial as the G-clamps and the H-brackets. Looking back over the whole period of construction, we used 500 metres of hardwood beams, 20 sheets of galvo and about 5000 f-words.

By Sunday evening, we had all the uprights in place, connected around the bottom with the heavy-duty skirting board. We'd also hammered some temporary stays in place, so that the poles wouldn't wave in the wind. Our old-man backs were hurting from lifting the timber, but we were amazed at how much we'd been able to achieve.

'That electricity idea,' mused Phil, 'I don't know who came up with it, but it's not a bad notion.'

←

Phil was busy over the next few weeks, but I made plans to go up to the block anyway, hopefully with Joe, so I could hook him into the building. The Delphi Bar may have been Joe's idea, but he'd turned 16 and was starting to be a reluctant builder. He was still interested in *mental* building — the sort where you daydream about lofts and staircases and the addition of huge verandas; but he'd become less keen on *actual* building, the sort where you stand in drizzle and wind, your boots caked in mud, carrying large lumps of wood until your back hurts. In the mix of Joe's life, his blues band was becoming the most important thing, and so on weekends he'd rather stay at home.

'But The Delphi Bar is your idea,' I argued. 'And now we're part way through building it. You can't down tools.'

And so, two weeks later, following my relentless bullying, he agreed to come up with Debra and me. As we drove up late on Friday night, he politely quizzed me about the exact time we'd be able to leave on Sunday. We discussed the possible tasks for the weekend. He didn't seem keen on any of them.

Maybe he had a point. None of the jobs was that attractive. Possible Task Number One involved moving 2000 mudbricks. Stupidly — well, actually it was Philip's idea — we had stacked all the mudbricks in the middle of the concrete slab. Philip — did I explain this was his idea? — had said this would mean the bricks would be close to hand when we came to lay them. The problem was that they were now totally in the way. True to the long tradition of the block, we had created an insane amount of extra work through the application of pure stupidity. We'd now need to spend a whole day of brutish, back-destroying work just to make up for an error of foresight. Philip's lack of foresight. Or have I already mentioned that?

Possible Task Number Two was the application of decking oil to the uprights, so they'd survive the months it would take to get the roof on. And Possible Task Number Three was the building of a retaining wall to contain the low bank carved into the hillside when we'd put in the slab.

Joe was noncommittal, shrugging in a teenager way. Then, once he got up on Saturday morning, there was the curious land effect. In the absence of other distractions — no TV, no computer, no electric piano — the idea of a retaining wall was starting to take a hold on his mind.

'I think I'll start at the corner and then work back,' is all he said as he wandered out. The next time I saw him he was throwing rocks into a barrow and pushing them up the hill. On our bush block, rocks were hardly in short supply; if they were a cash crop we'd long before have been millionaires. Debra mixed him a barrow load of mortar and I carried a few of the heavier rocks. Then we left him to it. He worked incredibly hard, entirely absorbed in the task, full of his own ideas about how to best build a retaining wall out of rocks.

Debra and I moved the ladder around the site, coating the poles with decking oil. From up above I shouted suggestions to Joe, telling him he should put the large rocks on the bottom layer, and go smaller as he went up the wall. His dismissed the idea and insisted on placing the big stones randomly, mixed through the height of the wall.

'It will make it more stable.'

He couldn't be moved on the issue. It was like dealing with Philip. Debra joined the debate. She went in on his side.

By the time he'd finished the first section I could see he was right. The weight of the big rocks helped fix in place the smaller rocks below. Joe had already learnt one of the lessons of the block: out in the middle of nowhere you can try out your ideas, you can have a go. Joe's rock wall was turning out perfectly, but if it had turned out a bit crap, I'd have shrugged and given it the usual: 'Well, it isn't meant to be the ceiling of the Sistine Chapel.'

Over centuries, so many words have been written about the joy of perfection, about the beauty of doing something well. And so few words have been written about the joy of the slapdash; of the liberation and learning that comes when you allow yourself to have a go; when you embrace the idea of doing a job that's barely passable. At home, in the suburbs, everything is meant to be perfect; every surface shiny. People spend a fortune on their houses and become intolerant of any flaw. It becomes harder and harder to feel that you can have a crack at something: what if you get it wrong? The house is an asset, not just your home. And so you end up feeling deskilled; a tradesman is needed for the simplest task.

Up on the block, you could indulge the opposite impulse, and discover you were semi-capable of all sorts of things — plumbing, roofing, tiling. You wouldn't do a great job, but it could be surprisingly passable. Providing, of course, you didn't expect it to be the ceiling of the Sistine Chapel.

Two weekends on and we were back, this time with Phil and Joe, who in his laconic teenage way, had expressed a desire to finish his wall. On Saturday morning, he again threw himself into the job while Phil and I began installing the perimeter beams — heavy

Phil and Joe build the roof structure of The Delphi Bar.

planks of hardwood that connect the uprights, right around the top edge of the building.

After we'd trimmed them, we needed to heave them two metres up, then bolt them to the poles. We'd already cut an inset into the top of each pole, so there would be something for them to rest on while we drilled the holes and slid in the bolts. But blind aggression and mad ladder work would be the only way to get them up. Joe, watching us carry the wood, suggested the old men might need some help. He added his muscle to the task, enjoying the idea that he could lift the same weights as the old guys. He then worked with Phil, starting construction of the roof frame while I passed up the materials. At the end of the weekend the three of us made eager plans for a fortnight's time. Joe was suddenly the keenest builder of all.

I did wonder how long it would last.

FOURTEEN

For the next few months we continued the weekend work — Joe always an eager participant. Most of the time he worked alongside Phil — the two of them up on the frame, bolting the wood together with metal fixing plates. He learnt how to use a drill, keeping the angle straight; how to use a circular saw without it jamming on the timber; how to nail down a triple grip. Then a slight hitch: Debra and I had encouraged him to sign up for a student exchange program over Christmas. He was going to Germany for six weeks and was not happy about it: he was going to miss out on the week in which we planned to complete the roof of *his* building.

Philip and I decided we couldn't put off the task. The Christmas break was a rare chance for us to whack on the tin — the necessary step before laying the mudbricks. We had eight days to do it. A proper pair of builders would do it in half the time, but then a proper pair of builders might have had some idea about how to proceed. We had no idea what we were doing. So much could go wrong it hardly bore thinking about. Listed in no particular order the major perils were these:

1. It might rain all week, never allowing us to get started.
2. It might start raining in the middle of the week, just at the point when we had covered the roof with plywood sheets but were yet to install the tin, leaving $1000 worth of ruined plywood sheets sitting wet in the sky, and much anguish below.
3. Phil might fall off the roof.
4. I might fall off the roof (less likely, since, due to my fear of heights, I would be spending the whole week searching for excuses to stay as close to earth as possible).
5. High winds might arrive making it impossible to handle the sheets of tin.
6. The generator might break down.
7. We might fail to bring the tools we need.
8. We might fail to order sufficient quantities of the supplies we need, in particular plywood, foil, battens, bugle screws, tech screws and guttering.

9. My fear of heights might dramatically increase, so much that I am unwilling to even stand in the same paddock as the roof.
10. We might fail to allocate enough time to the task, leaving the roof half-finished at the end of our nine days, with all our work destroyed during any subsequent storm.

Against all this I had one good idea. The original house had now been finished for years — except for one detail. The inside ceiling was meant to be covered in pine lining boards. Years before we had done half the job, working our way up from floor level, but had been defeated by the cathedral ceiling: we could never figure out how to get up that high. I considered hiring scaffolding, but the price, at the time, seemed too steep. So the job still needed doing.

Here was the idea: we could hire Willy and Colin, two local builders we'd already met around the district. They could arrive the same time as us and finish off the inside cladding of the old building. Meanwhile, Philip and I would finish the roof of the new building — knowing we'd have on hand a source of expert advice.

Willy and Colin rapidly agreed. They loved the high country and regarded the job as a weird holiday — the four of us, camped in the house, working our guts out every day and carousing at night. I nominated myself as cook for the week, hoping it might provide an extra line of attack in my campaign to spend as little time as possible on the roof. Phil made me promise not to serve baked beans.

Joe was peppering me with emails from Germany: had we calculated the right amount of tin? Exactly what day did we plan to start? Had we decided on the location of the water tank? There he was in the heart of European culture and history yet, like me, he was going to sleep each night dreaming about a desiccated block of scrub up the side of a smallish Australian mountain.

His brother, studying in Canberra, was probably having the same dreams.

I packed the ute ready to go. I had a length of drainage pipe, half a cubic metre of gravel, my toolbox, a generator, two eskies and an old bar fridge. This final item — I say with a blush of immodesty — was another brainwave: since the generator would be running almost constantly, why couldn't we also run a fridge? We could have cold beer all week. First a toilet, then power, now a fridge: slowly the modern world was limping up our side of the mountain.

Philip and I arrived on site and unpacked, plugging in our first-time fridge. We had one day before the arrival of Willy and Colin, and we spent it installing the last of the knee-braces — heavy wooden beams that tie the roof to the main frame. We worked all day at the job and it was a perfect example of the pleasures of building. Most of the time we were entirely silent. We tramped over to the pile

of timber and lifted a long, heavy section of hardwood —
Philip on one end, me on the other — and placed it atop
the sawhorses. Philip marked the saw-lines with a pencil;
I handed him the electric saw; he cut the wood; I carried
the piece to its new home. There was something
immensely pleasurable about this: dependent on another
person, watching what they're doing and responding to it
— but without the buzz of words which normally
accompanies a joint enterprise. It was like an intricate
dance, and there was pleasure in knowing the steps.

Once the braces were cut we fitted them to the
frame. Phil, of course, was up a ladder with his end of the
timber; I was safely on the ground. My campaign of
terrestriality was working. The beams were cut to an
angle at both ends, and any slight error could be shared
between the two ends to make for an acceptable job all
round. 'Good enough my end,' Phil reported each time.
'And good enough on mine,' I would agree. It was a neat
metaphor for the communality of the task.

Or on another occasion: 'I'm happy,' Phil said,
looking at the angle of the wood.

'I knew you were a dwarf,' I jumped in, 'but I didn't
know you were one of the famous ones.'

'At least,' he replied, 'it's better than being Dopey,
which is surely who you would be.'

At the end of the day we stood back and admired our
work: the knee-braces were installed as a structural
device, but aesthetically they added something to the
building: a sense of strong practicality, of clean, robust

lines. And to add to the satisfaction, I checked out the fridge: it was cold and so was the beer inside. For the first time in 25 years, we could reach into the fridge and grab an icy-cold ale.

←

On Monday morning Willy and Colin arrived, their two utes burdened with materials. Willy's vehicle, in particular, looked like the family truck from *The Grapes of Wrath* or *The Beverly Hillbillies*, materials strapped to every surface. I'd first met Willy and Colin a decade before, when they'd installed a floor of compressed mud into a hand-built house a little further along the ridge. They were passionate about bush building; particularly if the job was a bit odd and fitted their principles of longevity, sustainability and utility. 'The average life of a domestic building in Europe is now down to 17 years,' Willy said to me at one point, shaking his head in disbelief.

Colin came to building through pottery; he was of Scottish descent, taciturn but open-hearted, practical but full of ideas. Willy had building in the blood — his father, Peter Hall, was the architect brought in to complete the Sydney Opera House after the building's creator, Jørn Utzon, was sacked by the local authorities. The handover had been mired in controversy for years: some said Hall should have refused the commission; others — a growing number — credited Hall as the man who took on the impossible and brilliant dream of Utzon and helped bring it to completion. It was only in 2006, 11 years after his death, that Willy's father was finally awarded a medal for his work by his fellow Australian architects.

Just like his dad, Willy was here to complete the interiors. And just like his dad, Willy would have to work with some eccentric angles. In the Opera House, these were the product of Utzon's grand vision of a building made of curved shells; here they were the product of some dodgy framing work by me and Philip.

Willy and Colin unloaded their trucks and set to work, hanging bearers off the existing perimeter beam to create a rough platform. Already they had proved why they were the builders and we the amateurs: without hiring any scaffolding, they quickly had access to the high parts of the ceiling.

The main house may have been built with nothing but hand tools, but now we were using every available device. Willy and Colin had a drop saw to cut the panels and a gas compressor to fire in the nails. On our side of the site, we had electric saws and drills, plus a hired nail gun. The generator sat in the middle of both projects, electrical leads snaking in both directions.

While Willy and Colin trimmed their panels to size, Philip and I started painting: putting three coats of fast-dry acrylic onto our 30 sheets of plywood. The work went pretty well, aside from the moment Phil came across a red-bellied black snake curled under one of the sheets.

Gingerly, very gingerly, we lifted up the sheet and decided to award the snake full possession of that corner of the site.

The plan was to nail the plywood — painted side down — on top of the rafters, so that from inside you'd see the big timber rafters set against a crisp white ceiling. Foil, battens and then tin would then be nailed atop the plywood. We finished our painting by sundown and spent the night in the main house.

The old house was now a building site once again, full of sawdust and floating strands of yellow batt insulation. We hunkered down by the fire to eat, drink and talk, opening too many bottles of wine. Willy talked inspiringly about his dad, the controversy over the Opera House, and the thrill of his father's work finally being acknowledged. Later Colin went over our structural plans for The Delphi Bar and suggested a simpler way of connecting the guttering to the roof. Fewer materials, less work, better look. Thanks Colin.

Day two and the ladders came out. The top of the roof was about three metres off the ground; the sides were incredibly steep, the angle of a Swiss ski jump, and we had to find a way of getting our 30 plywood sheets up there and nailed off. Straight away I felt ill.

My fear of heights was not limited to building. On holiday in Europe, I'd visited Il Duomo in Florence and spent my time pressed against the stairwell, refusing to look over the edge. 'Can we go now?' I had said timidly to Debra after enduring 15 minutes of total terror. When bushwalking, I usually felt sick when others walked towards a cliff-edge to admire the view: I had to order them back from danger. On the other hand I was here to build a roof, and Philip could not do it single-handedly. To some degree I'd have to get over my problem.

We'd built a platform inside the frame of the new building so we could stand with our heads poking out at roof level. I started heaving up the sheets, trying not to look down. We slid the first sheet into position and then wondered how to nail it down. My nerves might not be good, but as the taller one — did I mention that? — I got the job. Teetering on an upturned milk crate, I reached out with the nail gun, up and over the rafter, my other hand holding onto the frame with the white-knuckled grip of the truly terrified. I got the gun into position and pressed the trigger, and with a bang the nail went in. The work was laborious and frightening, yet by the end of the day the plywood was all in place. Even better, the weather was holding. Two days without high winds or rain: up here, that was close to a record.

We had another good night with Willy and Colin, yet amid the lively conversation there was some unwelcome advice. Willy had been watching us work, constantly moving our rickety ladders to get access to the roof. We needed, he said, to build ourselves a scaffold: a wooden walkway along each side of the building. With the help of our nail gun, it would take us about two or three hours of work, but would then make every task twice as easy. He doubted we could finish the roof without it.

Phil and I didn't like the idea of wasting a whole morning, but Willy seemed to know what he was talking about. We'd do what he suggested, just as we had when Peter Stiff told us we needed to start over on our farm gate, 25 years before.

The next morning, Phil and I threw ourselves into the work — creating a rough-looking but secure work platform. Atop our scaffold, we found ourselves standing at the foot of the roof — ready to work with tools spread out at our feet. Willy had been right.

We unrolled a length of foil and stapled it across the lowest part of the plywood. Next we added the first of the battens — long strips of wood which were screwed onto the frame and onto which the tin is then fixed. Standing on our new scaffold it was easy to fix the lowest batten in place; after that it became trickier. To fix the second batten you had to climb onto the roof, your weight resting on the batten you'd just installed. No need for an engineer's report on the quality of your building skills: fail to fix the first batten securely and you'd never have the chance to fix the second.

Phil took easily to the work: he heaved himself onto the roof, standing on the first batten. He positioned one end of the second batten, and waited for me to jump up and push the other end into place. I pulled myself reluctantly onto the roof, hating every minute of it. While Phil was standing, I was crouched, my bent-over body pressed against the roof, crawling sideways over the frame like an acrophobic crab.

Not the roof of the Sistine Chapel ... the painted plywood has been hammered onto the rafters.

'I hate this. I really hate this.'

'Don't do it. I'll get Willy to help.'

'No, I'll do it.'

Somehow I managed to lift my end into place and inserted a screw. Slowly we worked our way up the roof, installing a batten and then using that batten to step a little higher. There was much drilling and screwing and lifting. Every now and then we climbed down in order to cut fresh battens; a rush of relief overtaking me each time my feet hit the ground. Seeing my terror, Phil suggested I take an hour on the ground, doing other jobs, while he clambered over the work, screwing off the highest section.

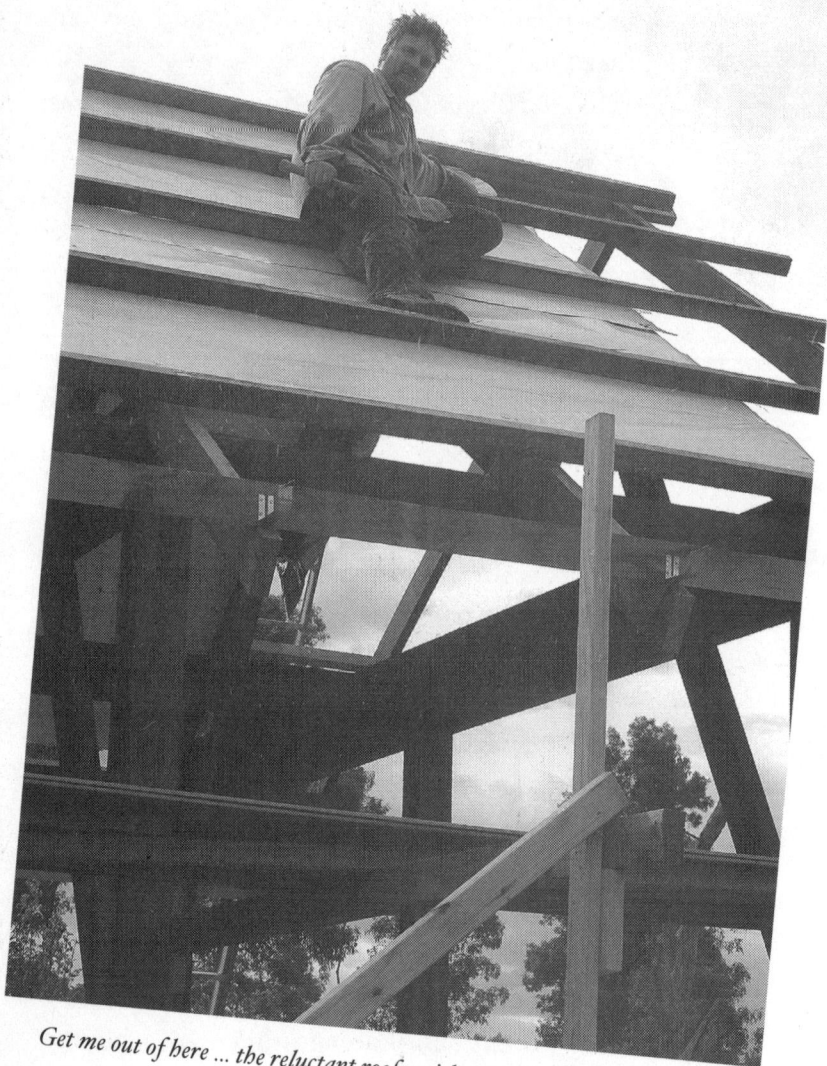

Get me out of here ... the reluctant roofer, sick with fear.

I spent the next hour digging a drainage trench. It was a mark of my terror that I relished every moment: shovelling gravel, sweat pouring off me, my back aching, the bits of gravel falling into my boots. But both my feet were on the ground.

Regrettably, I completed the job quite quickly and found myself back on the roof — Phil stepping easily between the battens, me stuck to the frame, gripping onto the battens for grim death. Somehow by nightfall we had finished one side of the building — fully battened off and ready for the tin. Just one side to go. When I went to bed that night, I found a neat grey stripe across my body, just under my chest. I'd been hanging onto the roof with such desperation that the middle batten had created a well-defined bruise — a mark of my fear; a grey stigmata of shame.

By 7am the next morning, Philip and I were back on the roof. I was starting, by pure gut-churning familiarity, to get used to it. Late in the day there came the moment when we were about to install the last batten. I was high enough to throw an arm over the ridge beam and look over onto the other side. I yelled to Willy on the ground: 'Quick — take a photo. I don't ever intend to be up here again.'

By Thursday evening Willy and Colin had finished their panelling and were ready to remove the scaffold and reveal the interior of the house. Philip and I, meanwhile, were on the ground, staring apprehensively at the horizon. We'd been lucky with the weather. Up to now. A southerly change was coming through. The foil was held down by the battens, but in some places it was starting to flap loose. As the wind built, Philip and I hopped back onto the roof and started securing the foil. It was deeply unpleasant work, up there on the frame buffeted by wind. It then started to rain. Lightly at first, then heavily. The foil protected the plywood to some degree, but it was not going to be a match for any serious weather.

'We're fucked,' muttered Philip. 'Seriously fucked.'

'It looks that way,' I acknowledged.

Over 25 years, we'd taken turns in optimism and pessimism, but we were finally agreed. It looked pretty bad.

Inside the main house, Willy and Colin removed the last of their scaffold and revealed a beautiful ceiling. The old house was transformed: the tree poles stood out against the new ceiling in the way that was always intended. The acoustics had changed too; suddenly it was like being in this beautiful wooden chapel. Just wait until I put on the Mantovani or the Hugo Winterhalter.

But outside the storm was gathering, the sky darkening, and the rain now coming down hard. Then it passed. The sky cleared.

'Actually it may be OK,' said Phil.

'Yeah, I agree.' Together again, naturally.

There was a final night of talking and eating; Willy agreed he'd stay on for a few hours the next morning to help screw on the tin. I realised this was a favour to me: he'd seen how terrified I'd looked all week. I'd also been

Quick, take a picture: a rare moment for Philip and me, together on the summit

The gutterman at work — any excuse to avoid being on the roof.

telling everyone how good I was at guttering. Not by chance — it is the roofing task that occurs closest to the ground.

The next morning Willy and Philip climbed onto the roof while I kept them supplied from the ground with insulation and sheets of tin. We set a blistering pace. I would feed them the materials, they'd heave them into place, and then use one or two screws to hold down the tin. Philip and I would bolt it all properly once Willy had gone. Within 90 minutes we had one side of the roof covered in tin. Within three hours the job was done.

As Willy came down, he apologised for the hysterical pace of the work. 'It's just I need to go home.' He mentioned his wife and young children, and the jobs that needed doing. But as he packed up, he conceded a more significant reason for his speed. 'I also just really hate being up there. The quicker it's over, the better.'

Ah, a man of my own heart. Just somewhat more noble and courageous.

The weather held. For the next day and a half, Philip and I clambered over the roof, screwing everything down securely. Due to my great skill with guttering, Phil was required to do most of the really high stuff. But in the end I clambered up there again and helped screw off the final sheet.

My fear of heights had been answered by a modicum of self-overcoming, and a whole lot of generosity from others. The job of roofing was complete. We had a cold beer. Did I mention the bar fridge was my idea?

FIFTEEN

With the roof on the fun could start: bricking up. We heaved the walls into place. It was fast, satisfying work. Dan came up from Canberra and Joe was back from his student exchange in Germany. Together we established a real assembly line — Joe whacked down some mud mortar, Debra heaved over a brick from the pile, and Dan expertly slotted it into place, tapping it down level.

Me? I was making the mortar. Did I tell you about my agonising rotator cuff?

The best thing? The boys had taken mental ownership of the new building. They would have long bullshit discussions about the improvements they planned for the place.

Joe wanted a rope bridge installed inside The Delphi Bar — slung from one end of the building to the other, but up high in the roof cavity. When I expressed my doubts, he looked at me askance as if I was quite crazy. 'Mum?' he said incredulous, 'don't you think it's a good idea?'

Debra was noncommittal. 'I think it's very creative,' was all she said.

Joe was also focused on the small sleeping loft in the new building. He reckoned we didn't need a staircase. Instead, according to him, there should be the sort of wall you see in an indoor climbing centre. 'It would make it such fun going to bed.'

Dan, four years older than his brother, had ideas just as grandiose, mainly involving underground bunkers in which valuables could be locked away, should we ever decide to purchase motorbikes.

'We're not buying motorbikes,' interrupted Debra.

'I'm just saying, if we were to buy them, it would be good to have a buried shipping container, with a disguised entrance, in which to hide them.'

Following three years of tertiary education the lad's grammar was perfect, even if he still had the fantasies of a 10-year-old. He also — and I found this incredibly moving — started using the same phrases about the place as I'd always used: 'It's great coming up here'; 'I start feeling a bit weird if I don't come up'; 'I feel like I'm myself up here'.

The place had shifted its use yet again. Part of its point by now was to serve Dan, who often came up with his university friends: the only sign of their occupation a tidy pile of Vodka Cruiser and Bundy rum bottles in the corner. Phil's daughter, Olivia, who used to be taken

Mudman: Joe at age 17, shovelling mud for use in the bricklaying.

Laying bricks second time around.

The brick wall of The Delphi Bar half finished.

down to the caves at dawn by her mother as a baby so she didn't waken the household, was now 18. She also had an enthusiasm for the place.

Joe, it's true, didn't stay quite as committed to The Delphi Bar as he promised he would. For him the craze came and went, doing battle with other enthusiasms, mostly concerning blues music. Yet by the time we finished, he had still built a fair chunk of the building he designed, including — with the help of his friend Ben — making the bulk of the bricks.

With all the action on the new building, we decided to spruce up the old one. For the first time, we installed mod cons such as blinds and a couple of electric lights, to be run off the solar system. There was still no TV, no computers, no phones, but surely there was no harm in a couple of lights?

For reasons dating back to the days of Denis the camp shower, there was a tradition of addressing objects by their name. The cheap hardware-store handbasin in the bathroom was similarly addressed as the Amalfi, as in the phrase, 'I'll just rinse my hands in the Amalfi.' We didn't say, 'Close the blind,' choosing instead the brand name of the new mass-produced item we'd chosen: 'Close the Torinos, will you, old boy?'

You could do an inspection report on the place and list all the things that were wrong: the slight bow in the roof line in the main building; the drainage problem in the sink; the badly laid tiles in the bathroom; the mild stink from the septic tank. Yet it was also spectacularly beautiful, at least to us. The architect and writer Witold Rybczynski has built his own house and says it well: 'The most beautiful house in the world is the one you build for yourself.'

We worked to finish The Delphi Bar but we took our time. When I was feeling particularly lazy, I would quote the Chinese proverb, 'When you finish your house, you die'. Building was enjoyable but so was just being there. We took the time to drive every so often into Taralga, which was enjoying a tiny renaissance: a few more people had moved into town. Someone had even taken over the old clapped-out pub and made it quite glamorous. The Wombeyan Caves were as beautiful as ever.

But I also loved just hanging around the block. I liked many things about it — wandering out along the road late at night with Debra, the white quartz of the road surface marking out the path even when everything else was pitch black; or waking up to a storm of birdsong, pulling up the blinds and lying in a pool of winter sunlight.

I also loved the effort, after a week up here, of making dinner out of whatever was left; and the associated rule that every fresh ingredient must be used up.

'You can't take that onion home.'

'Yeah, but we're having eggs on toast.'

'I don't care, you'll have to work an onion into the recipe.'

And who could forget my tuna mornay — a dish already close to the consistency of wallpaper paste, rendered entirely indigestible by the addition of a whole

The road past the block — not only beautiful, but great access.

packet of Italian cracker biscuits, 'just because they needed to be used up'?

And then there was the sleep after a day's building: muscles tired but head clear, you sleep, a sore arm slung behind your head, your whole body aching yet satisfied.

←

Dan was on one of his occasional trips home. We were heading up to the block, just like old times. It was late Friday night. I'd borrowed a CD from work which I thought everyone would enjoy — it was the Broadway cast recording of Mel Brooks's *The Producers*. I didn't only want my two young sons to enjoy the experience of carpentry and brick laying; I wanted them to share their parents' love of the theatre.

It was about 11 at night and we were on the tiny side road up to the block. I had the music turned up loud and was encouraging a singalong: 'Spring time for Hitler and Germany; winter for Poland and France'.

It was then I saw the road was blocked by a large truck. It was the piggers — guys like the ones in the Taralga pub who used dogs and knives to hunt feral pigs. Roped onto the back of their truck was the largest dead pig you'd ever see. The road was too narrow to get past, so I turned down the musical theatre and hopped out of the vehicle. I strode up towards the truck, my legs wide apart in a John Wayne swagger. In the darkness I spotted a bloke hanging around near the driver's door.

'G'day mate,' I drawled. 'Been doin' a little piggin', have ya?' I used a voice that was so ocker I could hardly understand myself.

'No, mate,' the guy replied. 'We're not pigging.'

He said this because the use of dogs for catching pigs had recently been declared illegal. 'Nah, we haven't got any dogs,' he added for good measure.

As if on cue six dogs bounded up, several of them kitted out with the protective breastplates used in pigging. I also noticed injuries on several of the poor mistreated mutts. 'They're just pets,' the bloke mumbled, weakly.

'No worries, mate,' I chortled, keen to avoid any conflict close to midnight on a deserted bush road in the middle of nowhere. 'The more of those mongrel pigs you knock off the better ... but if you could just move your truck ...'

He agreed and with that I bade him goodnight and strode back to the car, my bow-legged swagger getting more extreme by the moment. By the time I reached our car it must have looked as if I had some issues with incontinence.

The pigger moved his truck and I nosed our car past.

'See ya mate,' I said through the opened window, before winding it up and resuming the CD of musical theatre. It was then the laughter started. Dan and Joe had just witnessed what they believed was the most hilarious scene ever. They had seen their father pretending to be a bloke.

'Will you shut up?' I remonstrated.

'Ah, come on, Dad,' taunted Dan. 'That was pretty funny.'

'May I point out that I was the one who got out of the car and actually had a discussion with those fellows.'

'I think your father's right,' gasped Debra, fighting for breath through her laughter. 'I think your father is very brave.'

OK, they had a point. Is it necessary to put on a stupid ocker voice in order to be a man? Why didn't I feel I could approach those chaps as myself, using my own voice? The easy answer is: 'They'd punch your head in', but actually I don't think they would have. Most of my nervousness and anxiety is in my own head and always has been. It was unfair to blame these blokes for my lack of self-confidence; just as it had been unfair, years before, to blame my schoolmates for what I perceived to be their intolerance. The world, I now think, had never been as narrow or as conformist as I'd imaged it to be.

OK, maybe my issues with masculinity have not been completely resolved by my time spent building. I still see masculinity as some sort of protective disguise that I can pull on; out on a lonely road at night with piggers, I don't quite feel confident enough to just be myself.

All these years on, I remain a girly man. Building a house or two doesn't change that. I find it comforting to wear ribbons around my neck, like a festooned princess. I still think PJ Wodehouse is a hoot. I can't be bothered watching sport. And I still adhere to most of the values I acquired in the feminist collective of Canberra Youth Theatre. In so many ways I'm still the boy I was in high school.

But, truckloads of piggers aside, there's more confidence. Most of the time I don't feel I have to hide the sort of man I am. I'm quite proud of the mix that I have within me. If people think I'm effete, or 'not a proper bloke', I can toss my head, flounce off and mutter, 'Bet you haven't built a house with your own hands.' More importantly, I've realised that plenty of men have this sort of mix. That I'm nowhere near as different or as odd as I thought.

It's an immensely enjoyable realisation. Why did I have to wait until I was 50 to figure it out?

Maybe this is the great Australian secret (a secret a younger generation already knows): most Australian men don't match the ocker ideal which was sold as normality. At school, I'd always felt that I was not part of the mainstream; that I was on the outer. In retrospect, I now understand that nearly every young man felt like this. The 'mainstream' came down to a handful of guys — maybe five percent of the school population. They were good at sport, confident around girls and appeared to be entirely free of self-doubt. How they managed to be free of self-doubt is one mystery. The other mystery is how this five percent managed to convince the majority that they were the odd ones, while the five percent defined normality.

It was a mathematical sleight of hand, and it has taken me the best part of 30 years to spot the wonky logic. And to understand that it was acceptable to be myself.

It still seems to me that things we define as 'normal' and 'mainstream' are at loggerheads with the people I see everywhere, in all their delightful, sexy and eclectic oddity.

The Swiss psychiatrist Carl Jung wrote about the experience of building his own house in his autobiography *Memories, Dreams, Reflections*. He talked of his inner battles and how he explored them through reflection and intellectual hard work. In the end, though, it wasn't enough: 'I had to achieve a kind of representation in stone of my innermost thoughts ... I had to make a confession of faith in stone.'

It doesn't sound quite so grand when you are building with mud instead of stone, but the mud house was, for me, a kind of 'representation in mud of my innermost thoughts'. It expressed the tangle of things that made up my particular masculinity. It was my friendship with Philip given solid form; it was a physical manifestation of my romance with Debra; of the eager energy of my two sons; of all the friends who had helped over decades. There was also a certain hippy gentleness to the whole edifice; and a sort of blazing, violent masculine energy in the fact that it had been successfully built.

Jung again: 'I built the house in sections, always following the concrete needs of the moment. It might also be said that I built it in a kind of dream. Only afterwards did I see how all the parts fitted together and that a meaningful form had resulted: a symbol of psychic wholeness.' He was, he wrote, 'reborn in stone'.

My experiences are not entirely analogous with those of Jung. When Jung talks about building, he's not actually doing it himself. He's directing the tradesmen. Also, it's a lot more messy being reborn in mud.

I'd grown up obsessed with the theatre, uncomfortable with my own masculinity, a teenager who would flinch if someone used the word 'man' and intended it to include me. Then, in my early 20s, luck had delivered me a block of land, a best friend with some building skills and a feisty, chainsaw-wielding girlfriend willing to throw herself into the project. Together, over 25 years, we had raised two buildings on that bush block. In the process I'd learnt to enjoy the parts of myself that might be called 'manly': determination, heavy lifting, and a measure of aggression when a clout needed to be hammered in. And I'd learnt to find pleasure in the bits that were not at all manly but represented some different spirit in me.

By the end of the building work, a minor miracle had occurred: someone could shout 'Man', and I'd turn and say, 'You called?'

I made that house and that house made me.

ACKNOWLEDGEMENTS

I'd like to thank all the friends who helped us build: Belinda Chayko, Michael Cordell, Jennifer McAsey, Simon Cowap, Kathy Bluff, Mark Gronow, Michele Franks, Eli McFetrich, Ross McFetrich, Rene Vogelzang, Jurate Janavicius, David Chenu, Kerry Laurence, Eliza Laurence-Chenu and Ben Laurence, among many others. Ken Fleming and Michael Chalker helped me enormously with the history of the area; they are both great Wombeyan men. The team at HarperCollins were brilliant as always: it's hard to imagine better literary collaborators than Linda Funnell, Mary Rennie and Shona Martyn. Philip Clark and Debra Oswald both read the manuscript and suggested ideas. For instance: Phil suggested he should be taller.